LOVE:
That's The Heart of It

Antoinette Spurrier

Love: That's The Heart of It

Copyright © 2014 by Antoinette Spurrier

All rights reserved. No part of this book may be reproduced or transmitted in any form or by any means without written permission of the author.

ISBN: 978-0-9903824-1-6 (paperback)

The reason we so desire love above all is that there is a part of us that remembers the love vibrations of Spirit from whence we came and to which we someday will return.

*This book is dedicated to my Mother,
my life long best friend.*
MYRTLE EDWARDS GORDER

Contents

Acknowledgments... i

   I   Introduction...................................... 1

  II   The Many Forms Of Love......................... 3

 III   Romantic Love and Its Distortions 15

 IV   A LOVE WORKBOOK:
        Fourteen Steps to Acquiring More Love............ 61

  V   Be Someone Who C.A.R.E.S. 71

Acknowledgments

Collaborators

ANDREW FREEDMAN,
wordsmith who was the keeper of the intention; he expanded the book in scope, vitality and heart.

JACQUI FREEDMAN,
artistic contributor who captures Spirit and Nature in her light-filled watercolors. Her work is available through Jacquifree@yahoo.com

SHERRY (HEIDI) HALL,
the woman with the velvet voice and empathetic heart, who gave inspirational input.

DEBORAH PROBST KAYES,
proofreader, coordinator, sustainer, and multi-tasker with extraordinary tenacity and patience.

BECKY LAWTON,
provider of multifaceted contributions.

SURESH RAMASWAMY,
creative webmaster for FieldsOfLight.com

ANNE MARIE WELSH,
editor and dynamic catalyst for the birthing process of *Creating Deliberate Happiness: The Complete Guide* and this series.

MARK MURPHY,
aka Mr. Creativity who provided graphic art input and inspiration.

Special Mention

Myrtle Edwards Gorder,
Contributor of Original Art. Images are of her daughter, Yvonne G. Christianson.

The Foundation for Personal and Spiritual Empowerment
FieldsOfLight.com

The San Diego Foundation

My gratitude and appreciation also go to: Martin Anthony, Dr. James Ajemian, Rebecca and Todd Astill, Dr. Concepcion Barrio, The Bectold Family, Lou Bewersdorf, Wendell and Elaine Blonigan, Sheila Byrne, Renee and Sophia Carson, Cathi Eggleston, Joseph Escoffier, Susann and Richard Fishman, Paul Gorsuch, Norma Grey, Kari Kashani, Nikki Mann, Sandra and Geoffrey Mavis, Deirdre Maher, Alveda and Weston Maughan, John McLaurin, Patrick and Catherine McNabb, Anne McQuillan, Kevin McQuillen, Ron and Marlane Miriello, Dr. Carl and Chris Murphy, Chaitanya Narayan, Jim and Kathleen Newcomb, Brian and Alison Ross, Jan Saucier, Jeffrey Spurrier, David and Rose Spurrier, Ann Summa, Lisa Baker Scurr & Ron Scurr, Ricardo Torres-Roldan and Family, Penny Wing.

In Memoriam

John Laurence,
teacher, mentor and spiritual advisor. He was blessed with spiritual gifts that he shared unselfishly with others. He was instrumental in who I have become.

John McLaurin,
who personified friendship and sustained constancy, loyalty and love in that friendship. We journeyed together in the past and will do so again.

Linda Provence Diehl,
a beloved friend who expressed in wonderful ways both analytical thought and intuitive knowing. She made everyone feel that she had the ability to be mother to all.

Charles Mirandon,
who contributed through his friendship and loving support of our family and projects for more than 40 years.

Introduction

To the Reader,

My desire is to inspire you to remember that love is the very essence of your being; your destiny is to reclaim your true identity as a being of eternal love. You begin this journey by developing greater self-love, for there is no greater barrier to spiritual growth, romantic happiness or a fulfilling relationship than the secret fear that you are undeserving of love or that your destiny is to be hurt.

And so, I invite you to reflection and action by providing spiritual principles and techniques, including affirmations, that can help you turn this illusion of deficiency into a sense of your own great value. A workbook also offers practical tips and fourteen steps to acquiring more love in your life.

After covering the many expressions of love available to you, I dedicate a final chapter (Be Someone Who C.A.R.E.S.) to friendship, the bedrock of every mutually sustaining relationship. The topics surveyed are expansive.

- The real origin of love.
- The many kinds of love: self-love, love of family and friends, community and country, romantic and spiritual love.
- The connection between giving and receiving more love.

- Expanding self-knowledge and consciousness with introspection.
- Techniques to uproot negative self-talk and alter longstanding feelings of worthlessness that sabotage self-claiming and love.
- The differing perspectives on love by the Limited and the Eternal Self.
- Aligning the two selves to expand the experience of loving.
- Spiritual practices, including meditation, visualizations, journaling, introspection and especially affirmations, energized by will.
- Friendship, the ability to participate in reciprocal relationships, as the foundation of most successful adult love relationships.

My intention is to assist you in claiming your essential self as a being of love. As you better understand spiritual law and these techniques, you will attract more love into your life, eventually returning to your natural state of happiness, on the path to joy.

Congratulations on taking the first step!

Antoinette Spurrier

CHAPTER I

The Many Forms Of Love

KEY CONCEPTS:

- Love as a constant with different channels of expression.
- The real origin of love.
- The many kinds of love: self-love, love of family and friends, community/country, romantic, spiritual/God/agape.
- An invitation to expand your experience of love in all its aspects: self-love, familial love, friendship, spiritual love, and romantic love.

LOVE IS OUR ESSENCE

Our name is love. It is the very essence of our being. Though forgotten, our destiny is to reclaim our true identity as a being of eternal Love.

We desire Love because we are an inseparable part of Spirit—the Source and Repository of all Love. We carry in our soul the memory of that sacred Love vibration. We have come from Spirit and one day we shall return to our true home in Love's domain. William Wordsworth captured this truth beautifully in his poem "Ode: Intimations of Immortality:"

> *Our birth is but a sleep and a forgetting:*
> *The Soul that rises with us, our life's star,*
> *Hath had elsewhere its setting,*
> *And cometh from afar:*
> *Not in entire forgetfulness,*
> *And not in utter nakedness,*
> *But trailing clouds of glory do we come*
> *From God, who is our home...*

Love beckons us to awaken to the memory of who we truly are in our deepest core. By expanding our heart's capacity for love, we draw closer to that knowing. Love is inclusive, healing, forgiving, revitalizing. It motivates greatness, sacrifice, kindness—all the noble virtues of the human heart.

The desire for love is powerful and directs the lives and fantasies of most of us. Love also expresses itself in the love of family, children, friends, community and in a devotional relationship with our Higher Source, God. As relational beings, love is not only a transcendental quality that reflects our origin, true identity and innermost being, but also it is a universal impulse to merge in the intimacy of soul connection and union with another.

In this regard, love is essential to our happiness and joy. It is the melodic refrain to which we dance in the longing to belong and merge with the divine symphony. Life with love perfects the symphonic masterpiece. Existence without it is the source of all shadows and unhappiness. Behind all clouds of human darkness is the struggle to connect with others. Without love, there are feelings of disconnection from self, others, and from God. Behind all manifestation of evil's discordant notes is the perception of a lack of love and connection. To make the world brighter—to bring the heart into harmonic convergence—we must love more and know that our true name is Love itself.

> *Since love grows within you, so beauty grows, because love is the beauty of the soul.*
> ST. AUGUSTINE

Love Is!

We desire to experience and possess love to the fullest. That desire is universal. *Love is!* As an expression of the nature of the eternal aspect of our selves, it is constant and enduring. It is not tied to the waves of fleeting desires and the alternating emotional highs and lows that dominate the energies of our limited, finite, physical self.

Our very nature and essence is Love! We are on a journey to stand in the brilliant starlight of knowing this as a reality each moment, each breath. The nature of true love is to give, unhindered. Like the rays of the sun, love is accessible to all. When we are in the flow of love's sacred presence, its blessings flow unimpeded into our lives and, through us, provide comfort and light to others. Love is the universal promise. If we increase our capacity to share it, we move more deeply into our own nature. By loving, we create a doorway to the Infinite.

Love is recklessness, not reason
Reason seeks a profit
Love comes on strong, consuming herself, unabashed…
Having died to self-interest
she risks everything and asks for nothing....

RUMI, SUFI MYSTIC AND POET

Loving: A Lifelong Quest

But how do *you* begin to embody the magnitude of love? This is a lifelong quest that begins with knowing in your deepest core that you are lovable and can never be outside of love's reach. This knowing goes beyond mere intellectual understanding. The more you practice love in your life, despite your human frailties, the more you will experience it. It seems simple, doesn't it? Why is it, then, that we sometimes falter on this journey?

Love in relationship to another flushes to the surface all kinds of conditioned patterns—our deepest wounds, our grasping and desperation, our worst fears, our mistrust, our most raw emotional trigger points. To successfully navigate these often tumultuous waters, it is important to understand the deeper aspects of love as seen through two vantage points: that of the Limited Self, and that of the Eternal Self.

Love experienced by the Limited Self is, as its name implies, *limited*. Because it is conditional, it often involves the more negative human characteristics of control, duplicity, and its core characteristic, possessiveness. Its perspective revolves around demands and expectations. Possessive "love" is always looking for what it will get in return and has many strings attached.

Love experienced by the Eternal Self, on the other hand, is *unconditional*. It is part of your intrinsic spiritual nature and the origin of your soul in creation. It shines without limitation or restriction.

Divine Love is free and freely given. It knows not of strings or attachments, for it flows as powerfully, silently, joyfully and as freely as a grand river through the sands of our lives.

> *Do not judge yourself harshly. Without mercy for ourselves we cannot love the world.*
> BUDDHA

The heart centered in the Eternal Self has capacity that is never ending. As a connection to your spiritual energy, it supports the union of personality, thoughts and desires with your soul essence. It allows the presence of Divine Love—love without condition or judgment—to exist. Each of us is a conduit of Divine Love but we remain locked in our smaller interpretation of love when viewed only through the eyes of the Limited Self. It is our quest, therefore, to broaden our vision and to open wide the gates of love's highest expression.

Taking the First Step: Self-Love

We begin this journey by developing greater self-love. The more we can love and accept ourselves, the greater our capacity to love and accept another. We are also less likely to end up in unhealthy or abusive relationships. There is no greater barrier to romantic happiness or a fulfilling relationship than the secret fear that one is undeserving of love or that our destiny is to be hurt. Fears of inadequacy give birth to self-fulfilling prophecies because we tend to see other people as sources of approval or disapproval. Nothing we do is ever enough to give us the value we seek. We must turn this illusion of deficiency into knowing our own worth and value!

The more we are true to ourselves, on the other hand, the more we are true in relationship to another. This is an enduring spiritual truth. Self-love is the foundation upon which all that we most hope to achieve—in love and in life—will be realized. Out of it is born the qualities of compassion and empathy for others. We eventually outgrow the need to possess another or consider only our own needs. We become more available and have the capacity for true intimacy. In relationship, we desire only the highest and best for the beloved. The well-known Buddhist author and teacher, Thich Nhat Hahn, speaks of this:

> *Love is the capacity to take care, to protect, and to nourish. If you are not capable of generating that kind of energy toward yourself— if you are not capable of taking care of yourself, of nourishing yourself, of protecting yourself—it is very difficult to take care of another person.... to love oneself is the foundation of the love of other people. Love is a practice. Love is truly a practice.*
> SHAMBHALA MAGAZINE, MARCH, 2006

We practice self-love by meditation, affirmation, positive self-talk and self-care. Modern civilization primarily focuses on externals—one's appearance, financial status, education, etc.—and rarely encourages self-work and self-analysis. Yet these are vital to developing a stronger self image, and thus, more successful relationships. We must harness the power of our own thoughts and beliefs to change how we feel about ourselves. Our ability to maintain loving relationships comes from our *inner* maturity as an integrated, well-developed human being.

One thing is certain: We don't become more lovable by learning strategies to attract others to the "mystique" of our Limited Self. The real mystique resides in the Eternal Self. We become more lovable by understanding that *this* is who we truly are. It then becomes possible to recognize that same Eternal Self in another. Still, self-knowing, self-loving and friendship are rarely portrayed in most literature on the subject of romantic love. As a society, we have become addicted to outer appearance, which never portrays the true worth of an individual.

Self-Love is A Prerequisite for Healthy Relationships

All living things require love to survive, including ourselves. We must first attend to our own needs for love before we can love others. When we neglect ourselves emotionally, we become emotionally toxic and are not whole enough to give love to others. When we change the inner dialogue from the voice of the inner critic to that of the inner companion, we bolster our self-esteem and self-respect. Then we are free to nurture all individuals by being the caring, compassionate, thoughtful and kind beings we truly are.

Ideas of "magical thinking" run rampant on the subject of romantic love in no small part due to images reinforced in popular culture. The efficacy of self-work is minimized, or lost, behind the curtains of advertising, image promotion, and romantic fantasy. The difficulty with the idea that love is a romantic "happening" is that it does not recognize our capacity for personal empowerment, or our power as a generator of love. It also minimizes our ability to implement positive action through intention and volition.

Most people desire to experience more love in their lives without realizing the connection between receiving love and the capacity for self-love. How can we expect that another will be able to see the power of our light when that light is hidden from our own view? Do we believe that if another sees us more clearly and has the ability to know who we truly are, we will automatically get more love?

Self- love is about looking in the mirror and not assessing ourselves by the "if only" phrase. It's about accepting and loving what's there—including all our rough edges. It is necessary if we are to begin to penetrate the love vibration that is tied to our very soul nature. This increases the alignment and deeper integration of the Limited Self with the Eternal Self. We are love! We need to take the challenge and plunge, head first, into the vibratory field of Love that surrounds and embraces us at every moment. The love vibration within is ever calling to us!

As we learn to go beyond mere appearance, our values shift and we become more discerning about what really matters in a relationship. True compatibility can only be determined based on our natural dispositions, our real personalities, deep-seated mannerisms and habits. It can only be determined when each partner reveals his/her ordinary habits, peculiar quirks, eccentricities and other daily behaviors.

Our beliefs about ourselves and our worthiness, along with our early conditioning, are key to our understanding our aptitude for loving relationships and our ability to love another unconditionally. Let us take a deeper look at this aptitude through a series of introspective exercises.

Journal Opportunity:
Happiness and Love

When we think about happiness we often equate it with the quality of love in our lives. For some, love may feel as if it makes the world go around. Without it, life may feel empty, cold, bereft of comfort and meaning.

Consider the following questions:

- What is the quality of loving relationships in your life? Do you feel true love is a possibility or a reality for you?
- Can you be happy without experiencing "real love"?
- What does "real love" look like to you?
- Is your desire for happiness and joy strongly tied to your desire for love, both in giving and receiving?
- Do you feel that the source of love is external to yourself?
- No matter how much love you have, do you desire to obtain more?

- Is your experience of being loved dependent on the whims and preferences of someone else? Do you believe that others have the ability to provide you with or deny love in your life?

- Are you willing to entertain the idea that you are a powerful generator of love based on your essence and nature and that no one has the ability to take away your own power to love?

- What do you believe the connection is between experiencing love and self-knowledge?

- Have you entertained the possibility that, as you deepen your own self-awareness and self-knowledge, you also increase your experience of love?

- As you discover greater clarity and self-knowing, will you penetrate into the deeper spiritual dimensions within yourself and experience a sense of your true nature?

INTROSPECTION
Increasing Awareness about Romantic Love

Make journal entries around the thoughts and feelings that come up with the following questions:

- Is romantic love primarily a feeling state or an emotion?

- Is this kind of love an emotional attachment to another person?

- Is love fickle and whimsical? Is it easily acquired and easily dismissed?

- Do you believe that loving yourself has anything to do with your ability to love another person?

- What is your response to this statement: "Love is a state of being."

- Can there be romantic love without "chemistry?"
- Is romantic love subject to your control, in which you can extend or withdraw it upon command?
- Is romantic love a "chance happening" or an encounter with destiny and fate?
- Do you feel that you have ever confused chemistry and passion with loving? If yes, how has this played out in your life?

Discovering Your Beliefs on Attracting Love

- Do you see love as a "happening?" Is it tied to fate and destiny? For example, do you feel you just need to be at the right place, at the right time in order for those desires to be fulfilled?
- Are you passive in your approach to love? Are you waiting for love to "parachute" to your front door, arriving on the exact step that will allow you perfect access?
- Are you pro-active in creating love relationships? Are you an active participant: generating, attracting, giving and receiving love?
- Do you have any goals, or plans, regarding attracting love? If so, what are they? Do any of these goals involve self-change? Do you feel that your life could benefit by your becoming more loving and lovable?
- Do you feel that a deeper connection with yourself translates into a greater awareness of your powerful, infinite nature? Could it be that that awareness may create both greater self-harmony and a deeper connection with others?

Write your own definition of love. Take special note if there are areas you emphasize or de-emphasize. How much importance do you give love in your larger search for deliberate happiness and joy?

Write "agree/disagree" next to the following statements. Please also note which statements create strong feelings of agreement or disagreement.

- The idea of loving myself first is selfish: _____
- My emotions and feelings are separate from my ability to give or receive love: _____
- I need to make my own needs and priorities a priority and not let love get in the way: _____
- Love is primarily based on our biology or physical needs: _____
- Love between partners cannot grow without a sexual relationship: _____
- My ability to be loved is dependent primarily on how another person, or other people, feel about me: _____
- When I find an ideal relationship, I will be happy: _____

The answers to the above questions should provide important insights into the beliefs you hold about love and your capacity to give and receive it. The Limited Self may see love as a mere physical or emotional feeling, whereas the Eternal Self experiences love as an expression of its true nature.

Affirmations for Love

Riding the Waves of Love
Oh Father,
O Mother,
I call Thy name
But I hear the silence.
In silence
You ride the waves of knowing.
How I mistook the silence
Until I discovered
We were riding the waves of love together.

Divine Child of God
I give thanks for I am a Divine child of God.

Loved and Loving
I am Divinely loved and I am Divinely loving.

Heavenly Father's Love
I give thanks for I am loved unconditionally by the Heavenly Father.

Divine Mother's Love
I give thanks for I am loved unconditionally by the Divine Mother.

CHAPTER II

Romantic Love and Its Distortions

KEY CONCEPTS:

- The connection between giving and receiving more love.
- Expanding self-knowledge and consciousness with introspection.
- The role of the Limited Self.
- Introduction of the differing perspectives on love by the Limited and the Eternal Self.
- Aligning the two selves to expand the experience of loving.
- Using self-knowledge to align the two selves
- Friendship, the ability to participate in reciprocal relationships, as the foundation of most successful adult love relationships.
- To increase the amount of love you have in your life, increase the amount of love you give to others.

Romantic Love

A Red, Red Rose
By Robert Burns

Oh my love is like a red, red rose,
That's newly sprung in June:
Oh my love is like the melodie,
That's sweetly play'd in tune.

As fair art thou, my bonnie lass,
So deep in love am I
And I will love thee still, my Dear,
Till a' the seas gang dry.

Till a' the seas gang dry, my Dear,
And the rocks melt wi' the sun;
And I will love thee still, my Dear,
While the sands o' life shall run.

And fare thee well, my only love!
And fare thee well a while!
And I will come again, my love,
Tho' it were ten thousand mile!

Robert Burns' popular ballad persuades us that romantic love can be deathless, sustained across a lifetime "…I will love thee still… While the sands o' life shall run." This kind of sustained, passionate, romantic love does sometimes exist in those who have also cultivated deep, mature friendship, the very foundation of all successful relationships. Those who have a good relationship with themselves, who know who they truly are and who like themselves in spite of their imperfections—such people are capable of deep, passionate, sustained love that truly moves beyond the ego. That kind of romantic love is tied to love of self, and to the Eternal self, and brings joy to both partners.

More often, as we have seen, "magical thinking" prevails over realistic assessment on the subject of romantic love. The truth that love requires self-knowledge and self-work is minimized, or lost, in the swirl of media and fantasy surrounding us. The notion that romantic love simply "happens" does not recognize our capacity for personal empowerment, or our power to generate love. It also overlooks the positive courses of action we can take with our own intention and volition.

While love does flow through our human hearts and our biology as physical passion, it exists independent of our physiology. A relationship that is built primarily on physical attraction is often destined to be short-lived. Lasting love is based on friendship and the ability to participate in a spiritual union. That may exist with or without a sexual relationship.

Science has shown that there are stages to romantic love, attraction often being the first. But if a relationship is to mature, you must dig deeper into your inner resources of self-knowledge and self-love. Out of self-love all other relationships of love evolve because the capacity of your heart broadens to encompass self-forgiveness, trust, and appreciation. How can you forgive and trust another if you leave yourself outside of love's reach?

Your background and emotional history create feeling states that impact self-identify, self-esteem, worthiness and the capacity to love. Love can make you feel vulnerable as you begin to share your innermost self with another. If you start to care deeply for another, you desire that your feelings are reciprocated. Love exposes you to the potential for rejection, betrayal and abandonment. The full range of human emotions can and often does bring unresolved feelings and issues to the foreground to examine. The more you have worked on these with insight, self-love and compassion, the greater will be your capacity to open to love and to trust to another.

The ability to know and love yourself also increases your chance of *attracting* the right partners and friends into our lives. Sometimes, due to early conditioning, you may find it difficult to receive love and thus you attract, or are attracted to, unhealthy and unloving relationships.

Love Communicates

Many books have been written about the importance of good communication in relationships. It is vital that the lines of communication remain open, pliant. This requires skill and developing skill requires practice. All forms of loving relationships have, at their center, the ability to share mutually about common interests, needs, desires, struggles, and goals in life. When love is mutual there is a willingness to have open dialogue, especially when there are disagreements. It is the very foundation of a healthy relationship.

Maintaining open communication obviously requires ongoing attention and effort. Have you ever heard phrases such as "Love shouldn't be this much work?" Do you believe that love should be able to sustain itself without significant effort? A common misperception is that if there is love, everything else will fall into place. However, true communication involves respect for the other person as well as active energy on our part. These two skills are essential ingredients to making a relationship work.

A common assumption is that compatibility in romantic love is based on chemistry and attraction alone. This idea comes from the hope that sufficient desire, attraction, and chemistry will translate into a harmonious relationship, capable of nurturing and sustaining love with little work.

If only relationships were so simple! We humans are complex creatures, with many dimensions, including the spiritual. If we avoid the various parts of our nature, especially our soul nature, we remain imbalanced and unable to connect fully in a relationship. Anyone who promises that there is a formula for a deep and sustainable love that does not involve self-exploration, self-growth, personal empowerment, and continued effort is promising a love that will not be delivered. Our desires for immediate gratification will remain unfulfilled in the arena of love if we miss these components.

INTROSPECTION EXERCISE:
Romantic love between you and your significant other

Assess and evaluate the current romantic relationship in your life. If you are now in one, answer specifically according to that relationship. If you are not presently in a romantic relationship, answer according to your most recent relationship.

- Are you aware of "falling in love" with the idea of love? After the early infatuation period, do you feel that you are "falling out" of love and in need of finding a new partner? Has this been a common pattern for you? What is the longest period of time you have remained in one relationship?

- Do you see your "significant other" relationship as basically loving and supportive?

- Is this romantic relationship built on the foundation of friendship, mutual respect, honesty and trust?

- What is the usual emotional climate between you and your partner?

- What are the current behavior patterns that are occurring between the two of you?

- Do you feel that your romantic relationship is in a crisis period now?

- Would you assess your current relationship as toxic to your well-being and peace of mind?
- What needs to change for you to be closer to your partner? Are the changes you are focusing on primarily needed in yourself, or in the other person?
- Are you, or your partner, willing to explore making changes?
- Do you feel that you or the other person needs to have a disproportionate level of power or dominance in the relationship?
- Do you believe that your relationship can endure?
- Has anyone ever told you, or have you ever suspected, that you may have a problem with: a) emotional intimacy, b) communication, or c) commitment? Have you heard any of the same criticisms of yourself from other people in past relationships?
- Do you feel that your partner may have a problem with: a) emotional intimacy, b) communication, or c) commitment? Do you believe that others have criticized him/her in these areas in past relationships? Are they willing to explore making changes? If not, how is change going to happen?
- Are you prepared to stay in the relationship if no significant change occurs?
- Are you committed to trying to develop a relationship of greater substance that is based on the ability to have a deep, emotionally-intimate relationship? Or do you see your romantic life as being ever in movement, with changing partners and new, exciting conquests?
- If a relationship became less exciting, did you believe that only a new relationship would solve the problems? Did you

see the new relationship as the only solution to the lacks you were experiencing? Do you still feel that way?

- Is your present relationship based upon the promise of the potential of what it might become? How is that different from what is presently being expressed in the relationship now?

- Are you in an abusive relationship? Have you ever been in an abusive relationship before? Are you afraid to get out of an abusive relationship?*

Important Note: If you feel you are in an abusive relationship, community hotlines can put you in touch with resources and counseling that allow you to begin to take the necessary steps to change your circumstances.

All abusers demean, criticize, isolate, and insulate their partner. The self-worth and self-esteem of the partner is always attacked. The danger of an abusive relationship is that abusiveness tends to be tolerated in small amounts, and with time, the abuse comes to feel more familiar and the realization of the abuse becomes lessened.

Boundaries continue to be compromised, just like the boundary lines in the sand that are washed away by the waves. If this applies to you, remember that you *can* change your circumstances.

INTROSPECTION: LOVE AND CHEMISTRY

As mentioned earlier, physical attraction or "chemistry" often plays a significant role in the beginning of romantic relationships. This is the first stage, one that is important but that we also need to grow beyond if true love is to blossom and last through the years. It is essential, therefore, to step back and examine your beliefs about chemistry.

Have you ever experienced an intense romantic relationship in the early stages actually began to fall apart with time? Relationship experts explain how sexual chemistry generally becomes diluted over time. What if that initial intensity of sexual attraction and energy cannot be permanently sustained at that level? Many couples encounter difficulties when they transition from a strong initial attraction to a more stable union that involves routine and sharing all the dimensions of life, especially the practical.

Along with these questions, it is good to ask yourself how much physical attractiveness contributes to your idea of love. Is this attraction necessary for love to continue? We are trained from an early age to place high importance on appearance, but as the saying goes, looks are only "skin deep." How attractive we are on the inside—in our behavior and character—is often relegated to lesser importance. In addition, men and women approach this topic differently, with the majority of men being more visually oriented. Our upbringing also plays a significant role. The example your parents set for you in their relationship can make a stronger imprint than you may realize. Have you duplicated or imitated some aspects of their relationship in your own?

How you navigate these issues, and others pertaining to love, has largely to do with the degree of your self-awareness and strength of your efforts to live a conscious life. You cannot avoid this step if you desire to evolve in consciousness and become a fully integrated human being. As Carl Jung so wisely put it: "One does not become enlightened by imagining figures of light, but by making the darkness conscious." The "darkness" refers to those areas in our psyches that need healing, acceptance, forgiveness and love. Inner work prepares us, as nothing else, to meet the challenges and joys of a loving relationship.

LOVE AND DESERVEDNESS ISSUES

Habitual thoughts become powerful because of the power of repetition, not because they contain truth. They are energized by activity and deepen the grooves of mental replay by that act of repetition. In other words, negative thinking begets negative thinking and positive, truth-filled thinking begets more of the same. Altering ingrained thought patterns require systematic repetition of true statements regarding the nature of self. Only this will cauterize established mental habits.

Without conscious repetition, words or ideas of Truth will not be as powerful in reaching the unconscious mind as falsehoods that have been energized by the act of repetition. When truth is energized by mental repetition it will, eventually, create in its likeness. New thought patterns uproot the tenacious thought-weeds of self-negation over time.

> *Watch your thoughts; they become words.*
> *Watch your words; they become actions.*
> *Watch your actions; they become habits.*
> *Watch your habits; they become character.*
> *Watch your character, it becomes your destiny.*
> — FRANK OUTLAW

You deserve to be happy, to be joyous, to love, and to be loved. Your thought patterns are the great magnets of attraction/repulsion of energy which translate into our experiences in life. They create your circumstances. Whatever you believe you are entitled to receive—consciously or unconsciously—you will create in your life. That principle also applies to powerful alliances and romantic relationships. If you believe you are deserving of true love, you will attract those who are capable of loving.

Change your thoughts and change your circumstances! Change your thoughts and deepen your relationships!

If you look at the important people in your life, what do these relationships say about your deservedness? Relationships magnetically

Love: That's The Heart of It

> *If your trend of thought is ordinarily negative, an occasional positive thought is not enough to change the vibration to one of success.*
>
> PARAMAHANSA YOGANANDA
> *Law of Success*

attract your unconscious beliefs about deservedness. It is not God plotting against you that attracts your circumstances, nor is it a lack of God's love that creates obstacles. Sometimes the difficulty that presents itself may be the lack of your own self-embrace and self-knowing. *Self-negating themes and charged negative feelings or emotions around self are some of the most powerful energies that may incapacitate you in your experience of having successful, loving relationships.*

If you do not uproot these self-negating themes, life becomes a self-fulfilling prophecy. You attract the players into your life that confirm your beliefs about yourself. Examine more closely the themes around self-confidence and deservedness issues through the following exercise.

On a scale of 1-5, (5 being very strong self-confidence and 1 indicating inadequate confidence) how would you rank yourself?

- How would you rate yourself in terms of self-esteem? Self-reliance?

- Would other people give you a similar rating?

- What is your assessment of your worthiness, deservedness, and entitlement to receive love? Journal on these questions.

- Do you perceive yourself as lovable? Do you believe you are capable of giving love?

- Are you authentic in how you present yourself in a romantic love relationship? Do you feel you must initially pretend to be in love in order to have a romantic and/or a sexual relationship? Do you feel that you have ever misled or misrepresented yourself to another person in order to move forward in a sexual or romantic relationship? How do you feel about that? Are you insincere in your profession of love with someone in order to gain emotional or sexual access to them?

Are you capable of a long-term relationship? Does that include sexual faithfulness? How do you feel about sexual fidelity in a romantic relationship? Has that been a successful course of action for you in terms of creating meaningfulness in your life and closeness in your relationships?

- Rate yourself and the significant other in your life on loyalty, fidelity, and capacity for long-term relationships.

- What is the overall rating you would give yourself in terms of successful relationships? What is your criterion for success? How do you imagine others would rate you in terms of success in your relationships?

- Do you really want a close, emotionally-available, intimate relationship in your life? In living your life, what things indicate that this is true?

> *We all have a capacity to increase love—a capacity that allows our human worth to expand on a daily basis... Take a moment to consider that love can grow and expand within—whether you are alone or in a relationship. This is the kind of love you can feel for a fellow human being, spiritual being, child, pet, lover, life itself. It is the kind of love you give to yourself.*
>
> SUSAN ANDERSON,
> *From Abandonment to Love*

FURTHER INTROSPECTION

Do a written self-evaluation on how you perceive your capacity to participate in loving as reflected in these areas: Love of self, Love of others, Love of family, Love of community, Love of God.

On a scale of 1-5, assess your ability to give and to receive love from those sources listed above. Five indicates a high degree or capacity to be a giver or a receiver of love. One indicates minimal participation in giving or receiving love.

As you define your worthiness, you attract your circumstances, based on the law of attraction and magnetism. Your feelings around deserving to be loved are a reflection of core issues that came from earlier life experiences. If you feel you are undeserving to participate in a relationship in which you are treated with respect and appreciation, you will attract disrespectful relationships. The universe has an unending supply of people and circumstances that will coincide exactly with your self-assessment around worthiness issues. Feelings of being unworthy or undeserving of receiving love permeate every meaningful area of life.

All of us make mental, or verbal, statements that negate the experience of love in our lives. The first step in uprooting them is to make them conscious and to understand what beliefs they convey about us. In this exercise, write down any feelings that come up for you around the following statements.

- "I am unloved." (No one loves me.)
- "I am unlovable." (No one will love me.)
- "I am undeserving of being loved." (I'm not good enough to be loved.)
- "If anyone really knew me, they wouldn't love me."
- "God cannot love me. I am too imperfect and undeserving of His love."

Do you feel unworthy of having a full relationship with yourself, others or with God? Analyze if you are comfortable with the idea of romantic love, but uncomfortable with the idea of love between you and God. Or could you possibly be comfortable with the idea of love from God, but uncomfortable with the idea of romantic love with its sexual component? Do you see love of God as an unattainable love? Do you feel unworthy to receive love from God? Do these feelings create a sense of spiritual separateness for you?

All kinds of self-destructive mental patterns have been put into place from early life, perhaps when some rejection, betrayal or trauma occurred. We may not have been conscious of it at the time, but emotional walls were erected, all in the service of self-protection. A child doesn't know how to distinguish what it is told by a parent or teacher from what is actually true. If a child is told that he/she is slow, unattractive, or unfriendly, often those statements become internalized into beliefs as the child grows older. We carry these beliefs with us through life as tendencies, impulses, and internalized self-judgments. Our imperfections seem to validate our self-talk and serve to deepen these mental habits. Or we find that close friends fade away or commit an act of betrayal. Family relations feel stilted or perfunctory, or worse—angrily conflicted. All of these seem to confirm our unworthiness to be loved.

But are we really unworthy or undeserving of love? Could it be that this is a crystallized idea, formed by negative, repetitive thoughts and feelings of lacking self-love? What if you entertain more of the idea that you are deserving and worthy of being loved by another, others, or God? Is your consciousness able to participate more expansively in this possibility?

In order to create more peace, you need to monitor your thoughts. You need to be aware each moment if you are slipping into auto pilot. This requires a certain amount of diligence. If you uncover negative thought patterns, it is imperative that you disengage from identifying yourself with those thoughts, especially those that are critical, judgmental, or filled with "better than" or "lesser than" assessments.

As you claim the truth of your worthiness, you will expand your capacity to live in the vibration of love. You will attract more loving circumstances and individuals who also have a greater capacity to love. As you define, and most importantly *live,* you attract. As you believe, you are! As you change your self-definition, your life redefines itself accordingly. By redefining yourself and your life, you become an active participant in the creation of greater happiness.

A Comparison Chart on Love from the Perspectives of the Limited Self and the Eternal Self

Limited Self	Eternal Self
Conditional	Unconditional
Limited	Unlimited
Ego based and ego driven	Spirit-based and Spirit-driven
Relationship boundaries are necessary	Issues around boundaries do not apply
Desires include ownership and possession of another	Ownership and possession of another are unknown concepts
Conflict and tension restricts loving	Consciousness of loving permeates all conditions
Energy field includes excitement, anticipation, stimulation & imagination	Energy field includes calmness, peace, serenity & knowing
Passion is a driving force	Loving is an emanating force
Romantic love allows for greater stimulation & expanding	Love expresses in greater peace and tranquility without desires
Fluctuating desires and attachments result in discouragement	Steady, unwavering serenity results in expansion of love
May or may not have friendship as a base	Divine friendship is foundational
Impacted by deservedness/ worthiness issues	Unaffected by deservedness/ worthiness issues

Limited Self	Eternal Self
Expectations are never fully fulfilled. Discouragement results	No expectations exist. No discouragement results
Self-motives & self-desires creates transitory love	Higher, love-based knowing results in non-transitory divine love
Love restricts in negative conditions; perceived disconnection can occur	Love expands in both negative and positive conditions no perceived disconnection exists
Love is inconstant, altered and impermanent	Love is constant, unaltered, and permanent
Limited self-knowledge & ego-driven attachments create a restrictive heart w/restless desires	Self-knowledge generates self-love w/ empathic, limitless heart w/o restless desires

Understanding the Love Nature of the Limited Self and the Eternal Self

It is vital to cultivate the ability to love more, both in giving and receiving love. Love is tied to our happiness and our journey in knowing ourselves as spiritual beings. It is intrinsic to our joy nature. Love is the quality that brings response from both the Limited Self and the Eternal Self. And that is the power of love! Participating in love, giving love, is an act which aligns the Limited Self and the Eternal Self ever closer. *If we would create greater integration between the Limited Self and the Eternal Self, LOVE MORE.*

One difficulty in understanding love and how to participate more fully in that experience is due to not understanding how love is expressed by both the Limited Self and the Eternal Self. The comparison columns above should be referred to as often as needed until our understanding becomes almost second nature. In brief:

***Unconditional love is the expression of the Eternal Self.
Conditional love is an expression of the Limited Self.***

The Eternal Self is without expectations, discouragement, or disillusionment. The Limited Self has attachment of the heart with another, but that attachment is deluded by the ego's wants, needs, and desires that exist independent of the other person. To make this clearer, let us examine more closely love and the Limited Self.

Love and the Limited Self

The Limited Self, being driven by ego-based impulses, will pursue romantic relationships based essentially on ego needs and desires—"What is in it for *me*?" The ego, in its driving role, may be essentially undetected by the individual.

The Higher Self, on the other hand, always steers us in the direction of more Love, greater harmony, authentic ease, and true joy. Though the ego *promises* these desirable things, it simply cannot deliver them. It is not equipped to. It is important to recognize that your ego is the puppet of the reactive brain—the "don't-think-just-do-it" part of us that is in charge of physical survival. It doesn't take a long view—its job is to protect our physical body at the moment of threat. The ego or Limited self is equally short-sighted, territorial, greedy, fearful, and status-motivated, though it masquerades as being able to offer us all that our Higher Self offers. If authentic ease, joy, harmony and Love are what we would like to move toward, gravitating to the impulses of the Limited Self will not get us there!

So how do you differentiate between these two sources of input as you contemplate a decision—whether about a relationship or any other aspect of life? You pay attention to your thoughts. If they are fear-motivated, it's your Limited

> *The reason that ego and love are not compatible comes down to this: you cannot take your ego into the unknown, where love wants to lead. If you follow love, your life will become uncertain, and the ego craves certainty.*
>
> DEEPAK CHOPRA

Self. If they are greedy, it's your Limited Self. If they are status-oriented, it's your Limited Self. If they are territorial, it's your Limited Self. But if they are fearless, expansive, generous, compassionate, inclusive and harmonious, they are Higher Self-driven.

The Limited Self deals with struggles around attachment and the desire to possess. The excitement, stimulation and agitation of ideas around romantic love allow the Limited Self to participate in greater stimulation and greater imagination. However, it does not necessarily offer the experiences of greater peace and tranquility.

Most of us have heard others say that they love someone, but are not *in love* with them. Does that sentiment mean that sexual attraction and romance no longer have the power to produce the same level of excitement? Could the problem be that the excitement was never "love" in the first place? It is undisputed that attraction and chemistry initially can create the bridge that brings two people together. But if we stay at this level of physical attraction only, we may never go to the next level of deeper compatibility with a solid base of friendship. Physical attraction may complement a solid relationship of love. However, love does not cease to be when there are changes in the romantic aspect. This is only true when our consciousness is tied to the Limited Self.

The desire to possess another may be exalted by many as a high form of love. To possess is about consumption, conquest and ownership. This approach to love is always ego-based. The idea of "catching a mate" implies ownership and not true partnership. Partnership involves volitional participation where mutual respect and friendship are the foundational aspects of the relationship. The highest expression of love is demonstrated by the ability to honor and participate in the space and light of another individual. This sentiment is beautifully conveyed by the poet Kahlil Gibran: "Love one another, but make not a bond of love: Let it rather be a moving sea between the shores of your souls."

Marketing Love

The internet and social networking certainly have their place in society. But as in everything, there is the balanced middle path to experiencing the excessive bombardment with images that convey a fantasy-like quality of romantic love. In the real world, this type of love is simply, more often than not, unattainable and improbable.

You may lament the perceived lack of love in your life. You may even frantically pursue the goal of catching, possessing, and holding it. But once the goal is achieved, romantic love is subject to human inconstancy and fickleness.

Most of the marketing campaigns revolving around the subject of love involve ideas, products, image and merchandise. Marketing techniques around "capturing love" focus on the need to project the right image and "market" it. Adequate purchasing power is also assumed to be necessary in order to "find" love. To be "desirable" is to spend in our society. Advertising tells us that by physically remaking our image, we will have the power to capture and possess love.

Is it possible that obtaining love is not just about "finding love" via the right physical image and the proper marketing campaign? Is it possible that your own inner voyage of self-discovery has a significant role in expanding love relationships in your life? *The deeper truth is that your ideas create your reality. If you change your core ideas about yourself, you will change your reality, including the journey of loving.*

Self-knowledge increases the dynamic magnetism that emanates from you. That magnetism can change the positive flow of love into your life. Self-knowledge is the basis of self-loving. Self-loving attracts more and greater love into our lives.

When you chase love outside yourself, you reflect little on the treasures of love within. The pursuit of love becomes about grasping someone or something in order to feel complete. What is the true source of love, however? Is it dependent on another person or persons? Or does it manifest in and through people, and at the same time remain independent of them?

If the source of love is vibrationally tied to the creation of life and the universe, it offers another level of hope and promise around its access. Love is more than your perception of it. Perhaps *that* knowing can be better realized by the cultivation of inner stillness rather than the desperate pursuit involved in chasing love. In moments of stillness, you can glimpse the limitless ocean of love that resides in the Eternal Self—a love so resplendent, so deeply fulfilling that no words can describe it. Yet the Limited Self is often too busy with the pursuit and the adventure of capturing love to take time for inner reflection.

It may seem foreign that love can be found by cultivating an inner dialogue with yourself. This truth is more important and effective than the strategies of a "marketing" or external campaign—the idea that you need the best "packaging" in order to attract the right person. This erroneous concept of romantic love heavily emphasizes physical attraction and sexuality over the moral and spiritual character of another.

You may feel that only with the love of another person will you be complete and happy. Again, this reflects the idea that happiness comes on the installment plan when the perfect balance is achieved. This idea of romantic love does not involve a spiritual examination into your own nature.

A surprisingly high number of divorces are the result of excessive expectations of happiness being achieved through romantic love. There is a lack of understanding that romantic love must have a foundation in compatibility and friendship in order for the relationship to endure over time. This ability to achieve a state of harmony and depth of understanding can create a profound and meaningful love relationship. Your love relationships will have greater depth and potential longevity where divine friendship is entwined with love.

First, increase your capacity for divine friendship. Then your capacity to love and be loved will follow naturally.

Chemistry Can Obscure our Vision of Love

Chemistry, sexuality, and the urge for union are powerful themes in romantic love. The focus in this limited concept of love is the experience of attraction and attachment. It is the domain of desire. Ironically, you may find that physical or sexual attraction may actually be a deterrent from knowing the real nature of another person. Strong chemistry can deter the functioning of the analytical reasoning part of the brain.

You may experience the good fortune of possessing both physical attraction and emotional depth in the same romantic relationship. However, many relationships become more distant or end entirely when chemistry and physical attraction wane; they were never based on true love and friendship.

Life experienced through the Limited Self ultimately produces restless discontent and excessive expectations, which are the underpinnings of many failed or unhappy relationships. There appears to be no end to dramas, fickleness, illusions, and disillusionment around the subject of love when it is perceived through the faulty lens of the Limited Self. What you have always thought of as love may or may not be love in actuality. Many other experiences and desires may hide under the label of love, further adding to confusions and lack of clarity around its true nature.

Nothing is more idealized or portrayed as thrilling as romantic love. It is the embodiment of passion. It is the invitation to fantasy and excitement. It seems to promise the answer to all of our needs and to offer us enduring happiness. But can this alone sustain a relationship through the thick and thin of life?

Expectations that passion, feelings, and emotions, as well as sexual fantasies, will be forever at a high peak are rarely met.

The excitement and titillation of a romantic relationship often become watered down and doused by the routine of everyday life. Furthermore, the focus on sexual attraction and desires may negatively intermix with our own issues of deservedness, entitlement, and worthiness.

Managing our Expectations

As we become more aware of the unrealistic desires and expectations of the Limited Self, we discover that disillusionment is often associated with intimate relationships. In relationships, the expectations always, at one time or another, exceed our ability to meet them. Expectations pre-pave the road to discouragement and disillusionment.

The truth is that the difficulty with all new relationships is that they generally become routine with the passage of time. Without relationship depth, our relationships will move more into a state of endurance rather than cherished appreciation of our partners. Unless highly skilled, the Limited Self lacks the sufficient quality of discernment in the way it attracts and projects when seeking a compatible lifelong partner. Attraction does not disclose the qualities of another, nor does it give us clarity around the possibility of building a deeper and more substantial love. We may attempt to bury our disillusion-ment by courting a new love interest to feed the insatiable appetite of the Limited Self. But the insatiable appetite remains, and our happiness in love appears to be ever distant.

Romantic love, without the foundation of friendship, seems to promise so much yet frequently delivers so little. A relationship must be created that allows for someone who C.A.R.E.S., a subject covered later. This ability is pivotal to creating deliberate happiness in your life.

The potential is not the promise, and the promise is not the reality. The Limited Self has its identity tied to wants, needs, and desires around our biological nature in a physical/material world. Romantic love is tied powerfully to our identification with our senses and our physical nature. It offers the ideal playground for our imagination and fantasies. However, the romantic partner is unlikely to be understood from a non-ego basis. There is a tendency to objectify the love interest. Also, with the Limited Self, the desire to possess, own, contain, or in some manner constrain the love object from leaving, may be central themes around the idea of romance. That is the territory and domain of the Limited Self.

> *Of all the forms of loving, romantic love is most subjected to the domination of the Limited Self.*

Human nature idealizes romantic love. In the beginning, it can cast a beguiling spell of infatuation and gives a false sense of completeness which can never be fully realized or sustained. When self- love is there, you are much better equipped to discern what is truly in your own highest interest. You are better able to avoid succumbing to the enticements of romantic love and the Lower Self's thralldom to physical attraction and desire.

This is the first step toward becoming an emotionally mature partner. When people mature emotionally, they are less likely to re-enact or project past experiences onto their current relationships. They develop a strong sense of independence and autonomy, having differentiated from destructive influences from early in life. As they evolve within themselves, they are less likely to look for someone to compensate for shortcomings and weaknesses or to complete their incompleteness. Instead, they're looking for someone

> *Romance is the realm where we unleash our grandest and most delusional projections, where the shadow is sure to emerge in all its dark glory.*
>
> BILL PLATKIN
> *Soulcraft*

to share life with an equal and to appreciate independently of themselves. Having broken ties to old identities and patterns, this person is much more available to a romantic partner and the new family that they create together. Naturally, becoming emotionally mature yourself will help with this process and dramatically improve your chances of achieving a solid and rewarding relationship.

Inner Dialogue of the Limited Self

Some thoughts that express the Limited Self perspective are: "Another person will complete me." "My life is incomplete without a partner." "I cannot be happy without someone to love me."

Affirming a state of incompleteness by ideas such as these will only lead to more feelings of being incomplete. That incompleteness will intensify because it is being reinforced by a negative affirmation.

The danger of repetitive thoughts about incompleteness is that it can lead to a dependence on others to provide fulfillment. The myth that a "romantic relationship" will have the power to complete and fulfill us is a negative, unconscious affirmation about our state of incompleteness. This is both a culturally-based idea and spiritually untrue. "I am incomplete because I do not have a mate" is a false statement regarding the truth of our nature. Your soul nature has always been complete with or without any type of partnership. Such ideas, reinforced by negative repetition, will lead to increased feelings of isolation, separation, disconnection from oneself and others.

The Mirror of Relationships

Once we recognize that the world is a projection of our consciousness, we realize that true transformation comes from within, by shifting our own consciousness. The world is a mirror in every moment, in every situation, in every

> *Love consists of this: two solitudes that meet, protect and greet each other.*
>
> RANIER MARIA RILKE

circumstance and in every relationship. Each of us inhabits a private world, though our private worlds are enmeshed with each other's to create a consensual reality.

The mirror of relationships becomes an important tool for personal transformation and, ultimately, social change as well. There is one simple principle to follow: attraction and repulsion are both mirrors of our own self. We are attracted to those people in whom we find traits that we have and want more of, and we are repelled by those in whom we find traits that we deny in ourselves.

Romantic love is the playing field of wants, needs, and desires. Romantic love is also the playing field for expressing deservedness issues that will inevitably trigger the issues around worthiness and entitlement to receive. Your own unresolved issues will be reflected back to you in your relationships, whether romantic or otherwise. This is their gift to you, if you are open to looking in the mirror honestly. If you are caught up in chasing the "dream" of romantic love, as in a fairy tale, you are sure to be disillusioned. The more wisdom and self awareness you have going into a relationship, and the more grounded you are in the Eternal Self, the more you will experience the love you so deeply seek.

A more practical approach to the "dating game"

What really matters in a relationship? What are your personal criteria? Even if the ultimate source of happiness is not romantic love, healthy love relationships are vital to your well-being. If you desire to have a more meaningful love relationship, these practical steps may ensure greater romantic success for you. Try them!

- **Put Friendship First**: In a friendship there is respect, open-hearted sharing, trust, the desire to spend time together, to confide our deepest dreams, fears, and hopes, knowing that we will be received unconditionally.

- **Develop Self-Knowledge and Self-Dialogue**: Relationships of depth and merit emerge primarily from individuals who are strong in their relationship with themselves. No one makes a strong relationship with another person by diminishing themselves. Love is not only within your grasp, but it is within yourself. Be a friend to yourself first, and then be a friend to another.

- **Clarify Expectations**: Make lists of what you desire to have from a relationship and what you are willing to give in a relationship. If you are unclear about your expectations and desires around a relationship, then it becomes difficult to evaluate the potential. The idea that you will just "know" if the right person comes along, is, again, an idea based on physical attraction.

- **Be in the Flow:** Do not attempt to force, or coerce, a relationship. Create sufficient space for the development and evolution of the relationship. A date does not make a relationship! Dating is an opportunity to explore whether a deeper, meaningful relationship is possible and whether or not the relationship is worth pursuing. Focusing on sexuality intensifies themes around attraction. It does not provide an indication of whether or not there is relationship potential.

- **Communicate Clearly:** Assess and evaluate your "comfort zone" in initiating discussion about relationship expectations. For example, if you have been seeing someone for a significant period of time and you are clear that you would like to have a more committed relationship, do you feel sufficiently empowered to have that conversation? Or do you feel that having that conversation may eliminate the possibilities of an ongoing relationship? Is that about your fear, or is it an accurate perception of the other person's inability to move further in relationship? Prioritize improving your communication skills. Prioritize dialoguing. Be willing to express more of your thoughts and feelings. Many people may feel it is selfish and unspiritual to be sufficiently in touch with their own wants, needs and identity. People who are uncomfortable expressing their needs often come from backgrounds where compliance, obedience and submission were dominant themes.

- **Strive to Become a Better Listener.** Concentrate. Engage. Reflect back what you are hearing.

- **Be Certain of a Mutual Desire for Relationship:** Examine whether the person you are seeing on a regular basis is hesitant to acknowledge that he or she is in a relationship with you. Does your partner hesitate to introduce you to others, or do they introduce you to others in a manner that indicates there is no "real involvement" with you? If someone is unwilling to name a relationship as a relationship, assume that means they do not feel bound by the commitment, restrictions, and respect that would be demonstrated in a committed relationship. Also, consider it to be a red flag as far as relationship potential is concerned, if the person is willing to spend private time or intimate time with you, but insulates or isolates you from their social network. If someone desires a significant relationship with you, you will not be treated as if you were a peripheral appendage to their life.

Assess your options if you are dating someone and the relationship appears to be stalled. Your options are either to do something or to do nothing about the relationship. To do something could mean ending the relationship without discussion. Or another choice could be to attempt to open meaningful discussion and shared perspectives. Do you see yourself as an individual empowered to express your wants and needs? Then discuss your feelings. Lack of dialogue and discussion relinquishes your power. All discussions need to be respectful in acknowledging the perspective of both individuals. Another person is not a dumping ground for all your emotions, nor is it their responsibility to sort out all of your feelings. Greater clarity in who you are will allow you more appropriate discussions and the sharing of perspectives.

If the person you are interested in says to you they are not ready for a relationship at this time, be willing to calmly close the door and move on. If people are saying they are not ready for a relationship, assume they are not ready. Assume they know what they are saying.

Examining Your Assumptions

We often make assumptions about others, only to find that our perceptions were based on our own insecurities, fears or hopes. In relationships, making assumptions about another—their motives, feelings, behavior, level of commitment, etc.—can wreak havoc. Are you building a relationship based on false assumptions or accurate perceptions? If so, what are those assumptions?

For example, giving another person "more space" is not always healthy. However, if you assume that giving them more space will inevitably result in their moving emotionally closer to you, you may be sorely disappointed. Giving someone "all the space they need" may be interpreted in a different way by a romantic partner. It could be viewed as excessive independence, or insufficient interest. It could even be interpreted as indifference or detachment. Remember, without dialogue, assumptions have inherent dangers.

Common Assumptions Made in Relationships

Another assumption might be that excessive dependency is an indication of greater love. It may, in fact, indicate feelings of inadequacy or possessiveness, tied to feelings of insecurity and the perception that another person is needed in order to complete you.

> *If we learn how to love others, really, truly love them, not for who we want them to be, but rather for who they are—the perfect soul that God has created—then we have learned one of the greatest lessons in life...*
>
> PUJYA SWAMI CHIDANAND SARASWATI
> *Drops of Nectar*

Perhaps you feel that excessive jealousy is tied to love. This is another misperception. Excessive jealousy and control issues always indicate underlying feelings of inadequacy, insecurity, or being out of control. Controlling behaviors are not loving behaviors.

Remember that if excitement and passion are there, there may be a tendency to assume they are indicative of deep love. Not necessarily. They are generally the fuel of the Limited Self. It is the energy-infused Limited Self that is thrusting forward, attempting to claim new desires, new stimulation, and new attractions in an effort to achieve satiation that will never occur! By its nature, the Limited Self is never satiated and will always be left searching.

The only true solution is to realize that real love is expressed through the Eternal Self. It alone is capable of fully expressing its own pure nature.

We will change the love vibration and love experiences in our lives when we begin to entertain the idea that we are a container of love, a spiritual vessel, a divine being awaiting discovery.

In love relationships, the Limited Self has only three possibilities:

1. Attempt to maintain that experience of excitement, connection, and pleasure in the existing relationship.

2. Develop and cultivate a different relationship with increased possibilities of excitement.

3. Recognize that the heightened experience of connection, that sense of union and merging is but a promise of our spiritual potential. This promise will never be fulfilled without the cultivation of a deepening relationship with the Eternal Self.

Love and the Eternal Self

Love is the essential nature, and the expression of the Eternal Self. The capacity of the Eternal Self to participate in love originates out of the connection of the soul with the Divine itself. Love is not only the nature of the Eternal Self, but its direct expression. Love, as expressed by the Eternal Self, emanates from the well-spring of Being.

The Eternal Self expresses love through a higher state of realization. This higher realization of consciousness emerges out of the vibration of self-knowing and self-loving. This self-knowing and self-loving then emanates outward, increasingly unrestricted by the conditions of wants, needs, and desires which so stifle and entangle the Limited Self. Our spiritual light is enhanced by this higher realization. We become conduits of understanding, empathy, and compassion—uplifting our own consciousness and touching the lives of others as well.

Empathy Is The Movement Of God's Love Between Hearts

One of the highest expressions of love is empathy. It is the ability to truly feel (and care about) what another person is feeling. It is pivotal in our ability to transform from a merely self-conscious being to the consciousness of the oneness in all things.

Without a connection with the Divine, we are simply a biologically-driven organism in pursuit of continuing our physical and biological journey. With the understanding of our divine nature, we have the ability to recognize the Divine within ourselves and the divinity within others.

The more we embody our Eternal Self, the more we expand our capacity to love unconditionally. The capacity to express love comes from the God-created energy within us. Since love is God's nature, it is the essence of our own. The expression of the Eternal Self is the expression of the love nature of the Divine. Therefore, it never sees love as tied to lack or striving. Being unconditional in its nature, having a true centeredness in this vibration of love, it does not dissipate when the conditions of desire and attachment are not met. When this real love is fully expressed, there is no participation in self-motives, self-desires, and themes of self-gain.

True Love

"True love" is a term that has been corrupted by romantic notions, but its origin is actually the love expressed through the Eternal Self. True love is not contaminated by ego-based wants, needs, and desires. True love has the capacity for enduring friendship, respect, honoring, and cherishing another person. It is a mirror reflecting the beauty in your own soul. That beauty is there. *True love is a reflection of your ability to be a friend to yourself.*

If you desire to experience a deep and abiding love, you do so by cultivating your ability to see the divine within yourself, as well as in others.

Love expressed from this higher consciousness is unhindered by the attachment of the heart. Respect, regard, and empathy are dominant between individuals whose relationship is rooted in true love. This love neither ebbs nor wanes in its flow. Its nature is constant, continuous, enduring, and unaffected. It resides in permanence, constancy, and joy.

The Eternal Self As Expressed In Your Love Relationships

This journey toward the highest expression of love requires patience and commitment. You will not arrive there overnight, nor is it easy to conceptualize a love this grand, this pure, through the intellect alone. Like all of us, you have been bombarded with images of love as seen through the eyes of the Limited Self. Your consciousness is accustomed to experiences of love through the Limited Self. No matter how great your capacity is to attain the highest degree of realization and personal empowerment, you are still on a journey of understanding and experience. Conceptually, you can talk about the highest possibilities of life in the consciousness of the Eternal Self and you can read about the lives of others who have achieved this expanded state. Nevertheless, you move on your journey of self-discovery at your own pace.

If you examine, for instance, the spiritual figure of Jesus the Christ or many of the pivotal spiritual figures throughout history, you see that they exemplified the highest ideals of sacrifice, unity with God, and unconditional love. However, in your own life, those lofty ideals and behaviors may seem out of reach. Nevertheless, that should not tether your determination to continue to strive for a greater alignment between the Limited Self and the Eternal Self. Greater alignment of the two selves increases the ability to express and receive love more authentically. As the influential author of *Autobiography of a Yogi*, Paramahansa Yogananda, wrote: "Effort in itself is progress."

Characteristics of Love as expressed through the Eternal Self

- Unconditional love and acceptance of the expression of another without the need to alter or control.

- Love that is ever-constant and uninterrupted in spite of changing conditions or changing aspects within another person.

- The ability to recognize the highest qualities—the good, and the light of another—as a unique expression of divinity itself.

- The recognition of the right of another to pursue his or her own self-discovery. In such a relationship there is support and a loving desire to enhance the empowerment of their partner.
- The united support of two individuals provides movement towards eternal truth and greater spiritual knowing. The ideal is that two individuals join together in their journey of self-knowledge, self-awareness, self-realization by supporting one another in the uniqueness of their quest.

When we reflect on these qualities of a relationship, our hearts open, we feel joy, and the desire to experience love at this level seems very worth attaining. However, you may have difficulty visualizing and maintaining direction because of your human struggles and vulnerabilities. Perhaps you are unable to give yourself the compassionate understanding you need to heal the wounded child within. If you have difficulty embracing those parts in yourself, you will have great difficulty in learning to accept the embrace, understanding, and empathy of another.

Learning to embody the highest ideals of the love of the Eternal Self requires effort. But the goals of self-knowing, compassionate release of negating themes of the past, self-affirming and self-claiming, will unfailingly lead you to a higher state of realization and an increased capacity to express its essence and energy. Patience, faith and expectation are requisites on this journey; the reward is the love you seek.

> *Wholeness is not achieved by cutting off a portion of one's being, but by integration of the contraries.*
>
> C. G. JUNG

Some Affirmations that Express the Perspective of The Eternal Self:

"I am centered in the light and love connection with myself."
"I am whole in my capacity to love others."
"I am whole and complete, for I am connected with myself and Spirit."

Any statement that affirms the completeness of your soul nature will bring increasing feelings of completeness and connection. Affirmation has the capacity to create within a greater expression of love. It also has the capacity to create a greater alignment between the Limited Self and the Eternal Self.

As your Self-knowing increases, so does your capacity to align, attune to, and express (give and receive) love. As you integrate the Limited Self and the Eternal Self, you are able to deepen and penetrate into ever-greater depths of soul-consciousness, wherein all goodness, love, wisdom and happiness flows.

Love is ever constant. The avenues through which it flows are ever-changing. Love is constant because its origin is tied to the force of all creation. It is intrinsic to the vibration of our being. Love is one with the Eternal Self.

Healthy Love Relationships Require Boundaries

Although relationships grounded in full expression of the Eternal Self require no artificially created boundaries, people, still influenced by the Limited Self's erroneous ideas, tend to exercise either excessive or inadequate boundaries in relationships. Both extreme rigidity and excessive flexibility can create problems in relationships.

You may be unclear about your boundaries because you do not know what having healthy boundaries entails.

Positive relationship boundaries may be implied and understood, or be clearly defined and established rules, that allow for the proper flow of respectful interaction between people. What are your thoughts about boundaries? When you think of "needing your space" and another person who also needs his or her space, where are the areas of overlap and where are the areas of merging?

Clear and adequate boundaries allow each person to participate in unique, individualized self-expression. Guidelines and requirements for respectful interaction take the needs of both partners into account. Boundaries can be negotiated and renegotiated by open dialogue about the priorities of individuals and families. Individual goals and objectives have to be taken into account with the contributions of each individual considered. Boundaries can always be renegotiated! But respect and acknowledgement of the contribution of others must be a consistent theme in setting adequate boundaries.

To create such meaningful boundaries in a relationship, you need to expect respectful interaction and communication. If you are unclear about appropriate boundaries because you see them as unnecessarily restrictive, then perhaps writing down the thoughts that come to you regarding the priorities and expectations that you have in our relationships would be helpful.

Conversely, a lack of boundaries and too much freedom may be a liability to you and to the relationship because it may come at the cost of diminishing your right to express your voice and negotiate your needs. Your voice and your needs are deserving of both respect and love. Are you giving someone else too much permission to claim his or her own life without acknowledging the need to claim your own? Women may have more of a tendency to subordinate their ideas and desires in consideration for the needs of their mate.

All healthy relationships have clearly established boundaries. We may have the best of intentions by asking for minimal commitment from another because we feel that we are giving the gift of freedom. The danger is that we may unintentionally begin to eliminate accountability to ourselves and to the relationship. Accountability is a necessity for you and for relationships generally. Accountability may be lovingly cultivated by clarity in expectations, discussions and interactions over proper boundaries, and shared perceptions around realistic expectations in a relationship. Boundaries create avenues for expressing self-respect and respect for the other person. Respectful discussion, and the ability to hear the feelings and positions of another, are important in achieving cohesive relationships.

Love As A Masquerade Is A Theme Of The Limited Self

Themes of projection and self-healing are part of the disguises in the love masquerade. These common themes intermingle in our emotional life in a manner that is often mistaken for love. The Limited Self is ever in search of love and creates, often obsessively, some form of drama in the attempt to experience it. The strong desire to heal and experience completeness and wholeness may be the driving force that is operating through so-called love experiences. You may believe the goal is to be "in love," but often the unrecognized goal is to heal yourself through the agency of a therapeutic love found in another. Romantic love usually proceeds on the assumption that the source of love is outside us.

Some relationships originate primarily out of an unconscious effort to resolve disrupted developmental stages in order to gain feelings of mastery over trauma. Sometimes we are driven to select people in key relationships in an effort to heal these stages without conscious awareness of our process. In other words, if there was trauma in your childhood—if your parent abandoned you in some way —you may unconsciously choose a mate who has similar qualities so that you end up working on these unresolved issues.

Any one or more of the following themes below manage to intermingle and co-exist while becoming powerful catalysts in our creation of relationships.

Multi-Faceted Expressions Of The Limited Self May Masquerade as Love

The Limited Self may create love objects from:

1. Themes of psychological projection.
2. An effort to experience one's self as whole and intact.
3. An attempt to correct childhood brokenness by unconsciously replaying patterns or scenarios associated with trauma or damage.
4. An attempt to gain perceived mastery over specific disrupted developmental stages in childhood psychological development.
5. An opportunity to confront deservedness issues—the love object becomes a mirror. We select the relationships that we believe reflect our true inner worth.
6. An unrecognized longing to experience spiritual union. Unknowingly, we are in search of bliss union without recognition of that eternal call.

1. *Themes Of Psychological Projection May Masquerade as Love*

Psychological projection is a mechanism of the unconscious mind. Projection describes the internalized self-messages or themes that you "project" onto another when you are unconsciously displacing your own issues. These are themes that are within you, yet you ascribe to another without insight into your own psyche. We all believe that our themes belong to other people when in fact they belong to us!

Romantic love is greatly impacted by projection. That is because romantic love revolves around themes and issues of the Limited Self. Self-analysis and self-exploration are vital tools by which these unconscious themes of projection, and their impact and resonance in relationships, may be made clearer. With clarity comes power. To understand allows the opportunity to remove layers of cloudiness in your psychological self-understanding. This process of greater self-understanding expands your knowing and your loving.

That which we call love may be personal themes projected onto another or others. Another person, identified as the "love object," becomes the canvas on which we may project our own emotional and experiential themes and issues from childhood. These themes are internalized paradigms that had their origin in actual or perceived experiences of childhood. These experiences become entwined with self-identity themes and deservedness issues.

The value of taking back our projections is that we can now see and accept our partners for who they are — not what we wanted them to be; not what we wish they would change into; not for what they can give us; but who they are. The love that can now grow between two partners is profound because it is authentic and based more on the expanded love of the Eternal Self. True love, unlike projection, is a willingness to see and support another person to be their own unique, separate self. This will untangle us from seeking in them the perfect parent-mirror image of ourselves, for as long as we are still seeking to be completed by another person, we will not allow them their own autonomy.

2. *The Desire To Experience Yourself As More Whole And Intact May Masquerade As Love*

The effort to create wholeness within ourselves derives from lack of awareness that we already are whole. The Eternal Self within us has ever been whole and its nature is love.

The Limited Self erroneously ties a sense of wholeness to its linking with another individual. It is usually unaware that it is allowing another person's perception to define its worth. With that perception, your completeness is bound to the whimsical, alternating pulse of another's perception to define who you are. These fickle, alternating pulsations may obscure the understanding of who you know yourself to be and diminish the nature of love itself.

"Partnership" in its truest sense refers to two separate and whole beings — equals in their own right — who help each person feel their own union with the Divine within instead of through projective identification with their partner. As the love between them grows and expands to the entire cosmos, this kind of love gives each partner their freedom — the greatest gift of all.

Most romantic relationships are germinated and solidified out of the injured child and the attempt to heal while creating a sense of wholeness via another person. However, that person probably is also in a place of struggle with their own brokenness. They may, or may not, have insight into that, or insight into their own use of psychological projections. They could be projecting onto us the identification of a parent who abused or neglected them without any insight into that process. As we reflect on our own experiences with love, and an observation of other people's romantic love relationships, we notice how rare are relationships that are whole and that allow for the further deepening of the authentic love experience. Yet it is something very much worth striving for!

3. *An Attempt To Unconsciously Correct Childhood Brokenness May Masquerade As Love*

Trauma results in negative emotions and a psychological sense of the self as fragmented, lacking wholeness. Childhood trauma impacts the development of a strong central core of positive self-identity. The sense of "brokenness" also occurs where there is emotional disconnection from significant caregivers. This creates within the individual a sense of fragmented, or broken, identity with anxiety around worthiness to be loved. Another person who can love them is seen as the remedy for feelings and experiences of fragmentation.

It is the Limited Self that experiences childhood brokenness and is attempting restoration through a perceived love connection with another. However, that love connection may be the unconscious format to attempt to provide healing from childhood damage. The tendency within the individual is often to return to, or re-enact, stressful or traumatic events that occurred during certain developmental childhood stages.

For example, the adult child of an alcoholic may select a long-term relationship with someone else who is chemically dependent. If a person is chemically dependent, they are addicted to some form of alcohol or drugs, including the abuse of prescription medication. Part of the reason for the attraction to the addicted person may be the unrecognized desire to be "good enough" to be loved. Somewhere from the past there may have been a desire to be "good enough" to heal some chemically-dependent person, or the emotionally unavailable significant other. That "healing of addiction" which could not be achieved by the child is re-enacted in adulthood. The adult child of the alcoholic is attempting to claim wholeness and the experience of being "good enough" to get love by having a different outcome from essentially the same circumstances.

The difficulty is that the addiction had nothing to do with the child, or the behavior of the child, in the first place. The child in this case has a faulty core myth that basically states, "If I were 'good enough,' my parent(s) wouldn't drink." This idea becomes an unconscious belief that essentially states that the child, not being good enough, was the cause of the alcoholism or chemical dependency in the first place. The adult is now unconsciously attempting to recreate the familiar environment of chaos and emotional unavailability. These conditions are typical of alcoholic homes in which the child perceives not being "good enough" to get connection and love, and now is attempting to replay the familiar patterns with the expectation of a different outcome.

You do not have the power to heal another lost in their struggle of emotional disconnection or addiction. You do not have the power to heal mental illness. Many forms of mental illness have bio-chemical causes and are primarily tied to one's physiology rather than to environment. You were not the cause and therefore cannot be the cure. There is no way to be "good enough" to heal another human being. There is no way to be "good enough" to eradicate addiction, mental illness, or heal others incapable of emotional intimacy.

You do, however, have the opportunity to attempt to heal yourself from the bondage of false ideas and beliefs. You can free ourself from the circular negative energy of your thoughts that hold you in bondage. You are entitled to that freedom. You are being supported by the positive intention of the universe in claiming what is rightfully yours. You need to expand your belief to encompass the truth of your own nature and power. You must escape from the constriction caused from revolving and repeating negative self-statements. Negative self-talk and negative self-definition does not define you. These negative self-statements are the chains of your bondage which stifles your ability to create deliberate happiness. Such ideas serve no higher purpose, but they do restrict the light which is inherently your own nature.

4. A Desire to Heal Disrupted Developmental Stages May Masquerade as Love

As adults, we may attract romantic relationships with individuals who have similar characteristics of one who was a significant role model in childhood. If the relationships within the family, or with a caregiver, have been sufficiently chaotic, then there may be a disruption in the completion of specific developmental stages. This disruption creates a potential to replicate the past in some manner. We unconsciously re-create similar circumstances, or draw certain personalities, so that this time our experiences hopefully allow some achievement in mastery. It is possible to bring in enough sufficiently identical elements to recreate parts of the original trauma that never gained satisfactory resolution. These circumstances in childhood are powerful contributors to our self image and self definition. Simply reflecting on the areas of negativity will not necessarily release the energy tied to such self-definition. Confronting deservedness issues with strong intention to create change will be helpful. Expanding self-knowledge, self-analysis, and self-dialogue will also facilitate greater change and mastery over the past.

5. An Opportunity To Confront Deservedness Themes May Masquerade As Love

When we begin any new romantic relationship, we believe we are doing so to find love. We are not necessarily aware that on a more subtle level we are attempting to eradicate deservedness issues. The truth is that deservedness issues, if they exist, will play a direct role in the magnetism of who is attracted into our lives.

Behaviors that stem from deservedness themes (e.g. insecurity, excessive needs for reassurance, attracting partners who are emotionally inaccessible) become a mirror by which you may more clearly see how you assess your own worthiness for love. You cannot have strong feelings of unworthiness to be loved and simultaneously attract and maintain a relationship in which another reflects your nature as worthy and deserving.

That which we call love may be a vehicle by which we are attempting to move through our deservedness issues. The desire is to find another person who sees us as entitled and worthy to be loved in order to validate us as individuals. Again, this is an effort to heal ourselves. Unconsciously we know that the distorted deservedness issues must be uprooted. If we have not yet healed these issues through our own inner work, our negative thought tendencies will sabotage the potential for a healthier relationship. We end up attracting individuals who basically confirm our belief that we are undeserving and unworthy of being loved. Our fear will become manifest by our own unconscious process of mate selection and self-evaluation of worthiness.

We may develop relationships with people who are emotionally unavailable in an unconscious effort to heal the damaged psyche that resulted from an emotionally thwarted love relationship with a significant other in childhood. As an adult we may continue the "play" of inaccessibility through our current love relationships.

6. *An Unrecognized Effort To Achieve Spiritual Union May Masquerade As Love*

Most people who seek a romantic relationship are unaware of a more hidden desire—that of personal union with the Divine. The Limited Self may be forever in bondage to the insatiable quest for a perfect love that cannot be fully realized in human relationships. We do not have to live a life pursuing the insatiable quest.

> *Entwined in that state of attraction to romantic love*
> *is our desire for our own union and completion.*
> *Little do we suspect that part of our journey in loving another*
> *is about our effort to attain spiritual union*
> *with the Divine.*

Nothing in this world lasts forever — even the healthiest, most profound love relationships. Each of us will eventually leave this world as we travel on our soul journey to the Eternal. Maybe we do create loving bonds that we carry from life to life, still the permanency we seek in love, the desire to merge in a love that is without any end, can only be realized in the soul's relationship with the Divine. Therefore, the love you desire may be an unrecognized attempt to access that spiritual union. You may not know you are on that journey, but it is the journey of discovery that one day all of us will make. Your quest for that sacred union is tied to loving, or being loved, by another person.

The experience of union, or merging with another in the physical realm, may awaken embers of recognition of another "lost love" with the Eternal. You may remember a relationship promising union and the satisfaction of all desires. But desire will stir again because its home is in the Limited Self attempting satiation through the physical realm. No human relationship will quell the desire for true union. The perfected union is the union of yourself with the Divine and the experience of unending Bliss. The possibility may seem remote to your consciousness, but there are pathfinders who have made their way before you and have found the promised goal. If you place your intention on being a spiritual pathfinder, your sincerity will bring a Divine response. The road will open before you for the Divine itself will be summoned by your intention.

Romantic love may, for some of us, provide the deepest feelings of connection, union, and the experience of merging in a state of love. Love relationships have the power to awaken within the Limited Self another level of knowing, a distant remembrance of another state of joy, happiness, and union that involved merging into the higher states of spiritual consciousness mentioned in all of the world's spiritual traditions.

A journey into the layers of self will include heightened self-knowledge, the expansion of consciousness, and the opportunity to ride true waves of bliss as you deepen the experience of the Limited Self in union with the Eternal Self. Few experiences in life mimic the powerful, often unconscious desire that resides within us to know the ecstasy in love union and Divine merging. Whether you refer to the Cosmic Beloved in terms of bliss, or the embrace of the Divine Mother, or union and ecstatic merging with Spirit or the Infinite, we are all addressing the same, deep reality. We may not clearly remember that state of bliss union, but intuitively we know it exists.

> *The Divine call to remembrance is ever there. That love is the highest love of all. It awaits us always.*

STRATEGIES IN CHANGING PATTERNS

To begin to break any negative pattern and redefine yourself, you must first identify the pattern. In order to become emotionally available yourself, you must be willing to enter into self-examination, self-discovery, and self-dialogue. The art of introspection is the beginning of greater self-empowerment. The intention to change and create new patterns in consciousness is a stepping stone to empowerment.

If you desire love, you must begin by attempting to understand yourself. If you desire love, you must become a friend to yourself. If you desire love, you must become more self-aware and penetrate more into your own habits in consciousness.

> *Through human loving, we become acquainted with spiritual love and the longing for sacred union.*
>
> BILL PLOTKIN,
> *Soulcraft*

Affirming the truth of your own nature with the systematic use of affirmations will penetrate that truth deep into the unconscious. These affirmations will begin to eradicate the grooved energy fields of falsehood. Sound which is truth-based resonates at a different vibratory level than statements of falsehood. Energized truth has a unique power to begin to obliterate the sound and words of falsehood. As you change your consciousness around your deservedness, you will change the people that present themselves in your life. As you affirm your deservedness, cultivating, in time, the corresponding *feeling* that you are deserving, your consciousness will gradually embrace another level of positive definition. That change in self-definition will change the magnetism, circumstances, and relationships that flow from this change.

> *We are gathered here to travel together for a little while.*
> *Then in diverse directions we have to go;*
> *But if we have divine love in our souls,*
> *no matter where we go we shall meet again. . . .*
> *We can never remain apart.*
> PARAMAHANSA YOGANANDA

Affirmations for Love and Partnership

Relationship affirmation
By the law
of higher intention
and by the law
of magnetic attraction
my soul companion
is co-creating
a divine relationship
with me NOW.

Relationship affirmation
(by Paramahansa Yogananda)
Heavenly Father,
divine Mother,
bless me
that I may choose
my life companion
according to Thy law
of perfect soul-union.

CHAPTER III

A LOVE WORKBOOK: FOURTEEN STEPS TO ACQUIRING MORE LOVE

In your effort to create more deliberate happiness, you can take practical steps that will lead to acquiring more love. Who would not be happier with more love? Transformation, at all levels, ties to practical, serious attention to applying these fourteen steps to greater happiness and love. By attempting to apply these steps you create greater mindfulness about your consciousness and actions. This will create foundational change that in turn will unlock the love vibration and great awareness within you. Attempting to apply these steps will change your underlying feelings of deservedness and self-worth. The attempt will create a new level of access to self love and the love within.

So you are invited to begin the process of changing and creating new patterns, WHILE also increasing your understanding and perception on the process of love. As you experience this process your magnetism in attracting and giving love will change. Adherence to the steps in this process is <u>guaranteed</u> to bring more love into your life!

How to proceed

A daily ritual will reinforce each of the fourteen steps toward acquiring more love. Repetition accelerates foundational change and you are asked to repeat certain material every day for three weeks in order to establish habit patterns that reading and inspiration alone cannot create. By revolving new and positive thoughts in your mind, you will begin to create new energy grooves in your brain and new patterns of thinking and acting in your life.

Practice each of the fourteen steps for three weeks. Every day during those three weeks you should:

- **Journal** for fifteen minutes on the subject of that step.
- **Create a daily record** of your efforts to change by bringing that step toward acquiring more love into your life each day.
- **Choose and repeat an affirmation** related to that subject. Choose from the list at the end of the chapter or use the suggested affirmations for each step below. Write the affirmation on five 3x5 cards and place those in several highly visible places (kitchen, bathroom mirror, car dashboard, coffee table etc.), wherever you will be reminded to say the affirmation again. Repeat the affirmation at least 15 times a day.

This daily practice is at the heart of the workbook to accelerate foundational change. After 21 days you will have achieved a new level of mindfulness, choice, perseverance and empowerment by working with these ideas.

The Fourteen Steps

1. **Develop a more expansive relationship with yourself.** See yourself as someone worth knowing. For 21 days, journal,

record and affirm. Suggested affirmation: *"I am a divine child of God: Divinely loved and Divinely loving."*

2. **Become a better friend**. Be the friend you would want to have in your own life. For 21 days, journal, record and affirm on this subject. Suggested affirmation: *"I am a friend to all, for I see the divine light in all."*

3. **Develop the art of listening** to the things said and the things unsaid. Men, more often than women, tend to hear information as "solutions are needed." Sometimes the solution is the ability to hear in a supportive way without feeling compelled to give immediate solutions. For 21 days, journal, record and affirm on this subject. Suggested affirmation: *"I am present in the now. I am hearing others with clarity and empathy."*

4. **Be alert to your words**. Pledge to be discriminating in discussing your business and silent in discussing the business of others. Eliminate gossip from your patterns of speech and habits of the heart. The greatest danger in participating in the habit of gossip is the lack of centering it creates within yourself. For 21 days, journal, record and affirm on this subject. Suggested affirmation: *"My words are gentle conveyers of truth. My words are saturated with the vibration of love."*

5. **Plant seeds of kindness**. Every day do an act of kindness for someone for the purpose of giving, of sharing, or acknowledging. Weed out the motives of self-gain. Kindness always flowers into loving reciprocity. For 21 days, journal, record and affirm on this subject. Suggested affirmation: *"All my acts of kindness flower with the potency of love."*

6. **Develop the power of will and perseverance**. The quality of perseverance allows depth in life and relationships to be cultivated. For 21 days, journal, record and affirm on this power

of perseverance. Suggested affirmation: *"Daily my power of dynamic will strengthens."*

7. **Cultivate the habit of gratitude.** Gratitude, on the surface, may not look as if it is directly related to love. Developing gratefulness for the blessings in your life creates a consciousness where the positive is always being emphasized. If this habit is cultivated in small areas, it has the ability to grow into larger areas of your life. This habit has the ability to create deliberate happiness. Strive for gratitude around conditions, circumstances, and the qualities within the people in your life. The more we are grateful for the qualities, attributes, and presence of others, the more your behavior towards others will change. Nothing so cultivates love than the experience of feeling known and valued. Journal, record and affirm this continual cultivation of gratitude. Suggested affirmation: *"I am grateful for this eternal moment which I am experiencing now."*

8. **Affirm your powerful capacity to be a receiver and a giver of love.** Then act on that affirmation. For 21 days, journal, record and affirm your amazing capacity to accept love and to give it to others. Suggested affirmation: *"My true essence/is aligned with love./Love is the source of all./I come from that vibration in creation./It is the vibration of my participation./It is the essence of my name."*

9. **Accept the challenge of becoming a mentor.** Nothing worth knowing is too small or unimportant for you to teach. Lessons that have had a positive impact upon you are meant to be shared. For 21 days, journal, record and affirm your willingness to become a mentor to others. Suggested affirmation: *"I am a friend assisting others to the highest elevation of themselves."*

10. **Give the gift of yourself**, be a contributor to others. When you teach or encourage the blossoming of others, you become blessed, first of all, by that higher assessment of yourself. That assessment of yourself as a giver creates a change in your own consciousness in which you feel you are a contributor to change and you have the power to initiate change. Journal, record and affirm on this subject for 21 days. Suggested affirmation: *"I have the power to initiate and manifest dynamic positive change."*

11. **Believe in others**. As you give the gift of believing in another, you ride the wings of their elevation of consciousness. When you encourage the smallest step in another, you change the walk of all generations that link to that individual. For 21 days, journal, record and affirm your attempts to encourage others toward greater consciousness. Suggested affirmation: *"I see the divine light in another./ I see the divine light in myself./ I see the divine light in all."*

12. **Love yourself**. As you increase your capacity to love yourself, you increase the avenues, the channels and possibilities of expanding love in all areas of your life. For 21 days, journal, record and affirm about your effort to love yourself more. Suggested affirmation: *"My heart capacity is ever extending./ I am becoming the heart itself,/ merging in love with humanity, with myself, with God."*

> *Love alone is capable of uniting living beings in such a way as to complete and fulfill them, for love alone takes them and joins them by what is deepest in themselves. All we need is to imagine our ability to love developing until it embraces the totality of men and women on earth.*
>
> PIERRE TEILHARD DE CHARDIN

> *Love of God, love in all forms is the reaching of the goal and yet never coming to a stop. Power, when it reaches its end, stops and grows careful of its hoarding. Love, when it reaches its end, reaches endless and therefore is not afraid of spending its all.*
>
> — RABINDRANATH TAGORE

13. **Affirm your loving connection to Spirit** and to the light that underlies the universe. Affirming your connection to Spirit will expand love. For 21 days, journal, record and affirm your connection to the Spirit underlying the universe. Suggested affirmation: *"In all ways I am connected to Spirit for I am Spirit."*

14. **Unlock your inherent inspirational capacity.** Daily read words of personal or spiritual inspiration. Before going to bed, read those words again. As you explore the inspiration of others and are uplifted by thoughts, your own thoughts will begin to vibrate in more inspirational ways. This uplift will create in you a more inspirational person and unlock your own creativity. For 21 days, journal, record and affirm your efforts to unlock your own inspirational capacity. Suggested affirmation: *"I am inspired creativity. I am unlocking my inspirational capacity with love."*

Affirmations for Love

For Alignment with Light
I am aligned with the light.
I am expressing the light.
I am that light.
I am that joy.
I am that bliss.
I am that love.

For Connectedness in Love
I am divinely connected with myself.
I am divinely connected with others.
I am divinely connected with the light,
and the power,
and the energy of the universe.

For Knowing My Essence as Love
My awareness of myself is ever-expanding,
ever-grounding me
in the truth of my essence
and in the truth of my soul nature.

For Empathetic Union
I am empathy.
My heart
rides with your heart.

For Heart Expansion Toward God
I am expansive heart
bathing myself in love.
God is loving
through my heart.
And I am loving in the heart of God.

For Knowing My Soul
I am experiencing
my soul nature
in a divine relationship
with myself
and in a divine relationship with others.

For Experiencing Unconditional Love
I am loved.
I am lovable.
I am peaceful.
I am serene.
I exude the vibration
of unconditional love.
All are attracted unto me
for the magnetism is the energy,
and the strength,
and the power of God.
I am now participating
in authentic, quality,
deep reciprocal relationships
based on soul qualities and spiritual magnetism.

For Awakening to Love
I am on a mission from God.
My mission is to become Awake.
I am now Awake in knowing who I am.
My name is Love.

My daughter, Yvonne, at age 17.
MYRTLE EDWARDS GORDER

CHAPTER IV

BE SOMEONE WHO C.A.R.E.S.

To experience and to express more love in relationships, we must strive to expand our capacity for friendship. The ability to be a friend is tied to the attributes of caring.

KEY TOPICS ADDRESSED
IN THIS CHAPTER:
- The theme of capacity, meaning the capability of one individual to have an emotionally intimate relationship with another.
- The theme of authenticity, meaning a relationship based on genuineness and clear intention.
- The theme of reciprocity, meaning a level of mastery with the flow of give-and-take.
- The theme of effort, meaning intention and will are energized into a productive outcome of energy work.
- The theme of sacrifice on behalf of another, if needed, meaning the willingness to go beyond self-interests for the benefit of another person.

Co-Creating The Love Relationship Of Being A Friend

Paramahansa Yogananda, the great Indian mystic and teacher, stated in reference to friendship that "friends are God's way of taking care of us." True friendship, one of our primary relationships, is based on "mutual usefulness" as Yogananda describes it, and a respect for diversity and disagreement. Friends also mirror your self-statements, thus helping you explore your consciousness and journey in life in the company of others. Understanding the true nature of a relationship like friendship, rather than a romanticized or improbable one, can make you a powerful co-creator in all relationships, shifting your consciousness from the wounded past of feeling victimized to a fulfilled present in which you co-create the relationships you desire through the laws of magnetism and attraction.

Above all others, the relationship to be cultivated is that of being a divine friend. This is because divine friendship can manifest in all of your deep and meaningful relationships and even your more superficial ones. If you expand your capacity to become someone who cares, and expand above all the quality of your divine friendship, you will discover more of yourself, and more of God. You will share more, and the world will be changed by your sharing. The Eternal Self will shine brighter in those relationships as you proceed along the way.

When you begin to realize that the attraction of others into your life is a more active and creative process than you thought, hope for change can blossom. If you can move beyond distorted beliefs about your lack of deservedness to a clearer reflection of yourself as a dynamic, creative being, you will begin to create anew. There will be transformation in the old relationships and the creation of new relationships that can reflect another level of potential and promise. More of the divine spark and creative force within will emanate and express in your renewed relationships. You can begin the renewal with the vow to become a better friend.

Many books about being happier or having better relationships address externals—a more attractive personality, a better image to market. This approach is unlikely to improve your relationships because such attraction is based on impermanent and superficial aspects of the Limited Self. The relationships you want require deep, soul-centered qualities inherent in your Eternal Self. These relationships are ultimately more satisfying, but they also require you to employ your energies with focus and determination using spiritual principles and techniques.

Let My Life Be For Others: A Prayer

Let my life be for others
As it is for myself.
Let my days be the holiest of unions
With mankind
And myself.
Let me serve
For I am served;
Let me benefit
For I am benefited.
As another exists in need
I am needful;
And as his life shows bounty
I am bountiful.
Not one part may suffer
But the whole may perish.
Not one being abandoned
But mankind destroyed.
Let my life reflect my love
And my fellow man, my caring.
Let all be given in love
Or all shall be as nothing.

Most of us long for more connection—with family, friends, children, a life companion. It is both human and divine to long, at some level, for greater intimacy with another or others. It is our nature to desire connection, union, and to experience being cared for, cherished, and tenderly desired. To achieve more loving requires us to cultivate the qualities and characteristics of one who "C.A.R.E.S."

This chapter is about love and caring, not simply romantic love. Contrary to popular opinion, love is not based on feelings alone. Feelings may be expressed, but love is more than just a feeling state. To experience, to cultivate, and to express love, you must develop and strive to expand your capacity for friendship. The ability to be a friend is tied to the attributes of caring. Those who feel that the traits and expressions of friendship are unnecessary in romantic love often fail at such relationships. Excitement and feelings are the promise, but it is in the heart of friendship that love endures.

The way you live reflects in your loving, and the way you love impacts your living. Personal qualities and behaviors involved in meaningful relationships are applicable to all relationships. In romantic love, because of the emphasis on sexuality and feelings, the sexual "highs" are often emphasized, while character traits may be minimized.

Life, love, and relationships are not simply "happenings." Deep, emotional connections do not happen, they are created from the cultivation of qualities within yourself. You must invest integrity, trust, self-honesty and rightful intention towards others. The experience and expression of friendship will deepen the quality of your love relationships.

> *To heighten deep love relationships, we must increase our capacity for deep friendships.*

The capacity to love someone else is based, first and foremost, on an ability to love yourself. We benefit from examining meaningful adult relationships in this

> *It is a sweet thing, friendship, a clear balm*
> *A happy and auspicious bird of calm,*
> *Which rides o'er life's every tumultuous Ocean,*
> *A God that broods o'er Chaos in commotion..*
> *Its coming is as light and music are*
> *'Mid dissonance and gloom—a star*
> *Which moves not 'mid the moving heavens alone—*
> *A smile among dark frowns, a gentle tone*
> *Among rude voices, a beloved light,*
> *A solitude, a refuge, a delight.*
>
> PERCY BYSSHE SHELLEY

framework. Various character traits, qualities and attributes get revealed over time in all good relationships between caring individuals. Closer analysis of traits and qualities in yourself and others will allow you to evaluate more clearly whether there can be depth in certain friendships and other relationships.

The ability to enter into true friendship is a prerequisite for any enduring bond. All authentic relationships are based on respect, first self-respect, without which you cannot have an authentic relationship with yourself. And then, respect for others. Respect underpins caring and love and there cannot be love and caring without friendship. Respect is also the basis for trust. And without trust, no one can establish real depth in a relationship. Respect also involves a capacity for reverence, the ability to honor the light shining from another human being.

The foundation of love is an authentic, caring relationship in which both individuals show their ability to engage in a reciprocal relationship. Friendship requires giving and receiving, and the whole notion of friendship needs to be elevated to a high level of respect and attention, for being a true friend allows access to the divine.

Love: That's The Heart of It

Ideally, both friends demonstrate a capacity to sacrifice for the other beyond the narrow interests of self, which are always tied to the Limited Self. The ability to sacrifice for another is always tied to the Eternal Self.

Self-analysis and self-dialogue, utilizing the acronym **C.A.R.E.S.** may assist us in assessing traits that are important in all relationships.

- **C**apacity, meaning the capability of one individual to have an emotionally intimate relationship with another.
- **A**uthenticity, meaning a relationship based on genuineness and clear intention.
- **R**eciprocity, meaning a level of mastery with the flow of give-and-take.
- **E**ffort, meaning intention and will are energized into a productive outcome.
- **S**acrifice on behalf of another, if needed; the willingness to go beyond self-interests for the benefit of another person.

C.A.R.E. is involved in love. C.A.R.E. is involved in liking. C.A.R.E. is involved in friendship. Become someone who C.A.R.E.S

The Acronym C.A.R.E.S.—a Tool for Self-Assessment

Capacity

Authenticity

Reciprocity

Effort

Sacrifice

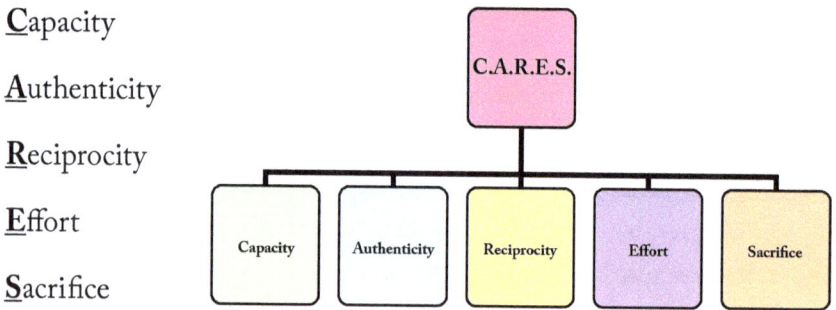

The qualities referred to in the acronym C.A.R.E.S. are the foundation of all meaningful relationships. They are expressed in deep friendships, as well as other love relationships.

The word "care" has less of an emotional charge than "love." But to care <u>is</u> to love, for there is no love if there is not caring. There is no love, if there is no respect, or genuineness. There is no love, if the consciousness is tied excessively to self-interests, selfish desires and objectives. One reason so few love relationships are sustained over time is that too little friendship is involved. If we use the word "care" as an acronym, and use it in self-assessment, it may prove to be a useful tool in increasing our capacity for caring and therefore, loving.

CAPACITY

The word "capacity," in this context, is the sustained, demonstrated ability to participate in the give and take of meaningful relationships. It is the ability, over time, to have stability and commitment in an ongoing relationship through accountability, adjustment, and compromise. It embraces friendship. The relationship is seen and valued as worthy of adjustments, assessments, prioritizing, reprioritizing, and negotiating. Capacity involves going beyond simply meeting personal needs to the willingness to compromise. The relationship becomes enhanced by reciprocity. To determine your capacity for healthy relationships, you may:

1. Assess <u>yourself</u> in terms of how fully you can participate in meaningful, loving relationships over time.
2. Assess the <u>other person</u>, or other people, in terms of their capacity to participate in loving relationships over time.

In assessing capacity, pay attention to:
- Relationship history (nature and duration).
- Relationship patterns over time.

- Tendency towards short-term or long-term relationships.
- Consistency between the "walk" and the "talk." (Distinguish between what people say and what people do.)
- The ability to be a good friend over time.
- Tendencies toward chemical dependency or addiction.
- History of emotional instability or psychiatric disturbance.

If you wish to more fully explore some of these areas, explanations of each of them, and a series of questions, appear in Appendix A.

You may think that someone lacking the capacity for an emotionally intimate relationship is going to magically acquire it with the passage of time or because of your love. As described earlier, what you believe is the promise and potential of another can simply be projected wants, needs, and desires. You may see yourself as unworthy or inadequate, but neither your perception, nor the perception of others, actually reflect your value and worth. You may also feel that having hope about another person's ability to change will make change happen. Only another person's commitment, expressed intention and energized will can create notable change over time.

AUTHENTICITY

To be authentic is to be genuine with yourself and with others. In order to do so, your two natures must be aligned, and aligned with truth. There must be truth and consistency between the "walk and the talk" of any authentic individual.

Do People Know Your "Real" Nature?

Do you project to others your "real" self? Are you cautious in revealing that? Perhaps you hide behind the roles you play, or present yourself chameleon-like according to what you believe others may want. If you project changing selves to others, is it because you are uncertain about how you will be received or are you unclear about who you are?

You are the artist who is painting the picture of yourself, and the actor scripting the roles you play. What is positive in your image projections? What would you like to change? Perhaps you worry that

> *An authentic relationship is a Spirit-filled relationship with self and with others. Its foundation is truth and its words, actions, and deeds are motivated by genuineness with regard and respect for others.*

when someone comes to know you that they will be unable to love you. Perhaps you hide aspects of yourself and keep people at a distance in order to have a safe experience of love. Distance creates disconnection and lessens communication. Thus intimacy is sacrificed. Distant relationships are not safe, but rather empty and void of meaning.

You can move toward greater authenticity if you are willing to make the effort of consciousness exploration and self-dialogue. A relationship in which you lack harmony with yourself and others cannot be authentic, so you must be vigilant in paying attention to the goal of centeredness within. A greater alignment with truth and your own nature is the root from which an authentic relationship can blossom. Steps toward authenticity include:

- Honest self-dialogue.
- Self-exploration, which results in greater knowing, for such knowing results in self-acceptance and the ability to embark on change.
- Confronting your fears! As you name your fears you empower yourself to become victorious over them.
- Identifying and uprooting faulty themes of deservedness.
- Striving to better integrate the Limited and Eternal Selves.

As you move toward the vibration and experience of inner truth, your need to defend your actions will diminish. The diminishing of defensive postures will allow less fear-bound and shame-filled actions. The fear of exposure and disclosure limits your self-expression and the embrace of others. The more honest you are with yourself, the more you will be able to have an authentic relationship with yourself and others.

An authentic relationship is aligned with Truth and operates from the place of the highest good for the self and others. An authentic relationship cannot exist where motives of manipulation, self-gain, and self-promotion exist at the expense of another. Remember, it is not possible to correct a lack of authenticity in another person by inspiring, instructing, or "loving enough" to transform them.

Authenticity in interactions with others emerges out of the ability to be centered within. Authenticity requires that at a deep, interior level you are aligned with Truth. The more you commit to discovering the Eternal Self, the greater will be your alignment.

Going Deeper: Authentic Relationship Checklist

Journal on these ideas to be more in touch with your own feelings about the authenticity of your relationships.

- Rate your own relationships on a scale of 1-5, with 5 being most authentic. How do you rate your friendships? Your relationships with family, including children? Your relationships with significant others? With your spiritual community? Your marital partner?

- Is your relationship with your parents and siblings a more authentic relationship than your relationship with your mate and your children? Which is the more authentic relationship, and why?

- In general, are your relationships genuine and real, or superficial? How does the idea of an authentic relationship fit into your love relationships in general? How does it fit in with the romantic relationship in your life?

- Where does love of self fit into your assessment of an authentic relationship? If you do not love yourself, from what wellspring of genuineness can you comfortably participate? Do you participate less authentically in different types of love relationships?

- Do you feel you have an authentic relationship with God? Or is fear and the concern over punishment a more overriding feeling than love in your relationship with God?

RECIPROCITY

For our purposes, a reciprocal relationship involves a high degree of mastery in the flow of give and take between individuals. Built on a foundation of respect, such a relationship involves each individual's ability to hear the position of the other. Communication and negotiation are strong in a reciprocal relationship. The wants and needs of others, as well as ourselves, are addressed during the ebb and flow of giving and receiving. Developing the ability to hear the thoughts and feelings of others will expand your potential for both capacity and reciprocity.

A reciprocal relationship does not involve dominance and control. Nor does it involve subordination or loss of identity in order to accommodate the expectations of another. In a reciprocal relationship, both individuals work to give loving

> *Fear immobilizes us. It freezes us. It prevents us from thinking clearly. Most of all it serves no purpose. No tragedy has ever been prevented by fear. No, calm serene, wise understanding coupled with undying faith is what is needed.*
>
> SWAMI SATCHIDANAND SARASWATI

support to each other's desires and responsibilities. The commitment to one another becomes a bridge of living, loving support.

Self-dialogue and communication with others is necessary for there to be a reciprocal relationship. Without communication there is no clarity about wants, needs, and desires. Communication encourages both discussion and negotiation, yet each of us has a different style of communication and negotiation. If there is a tendency to want to dominate with your ideas, you lose that capacity for reciprocity. You must see the ideas of the people in each of your different relationships as equally important and equally valid.

A reciprocal relationship also originates from a strong sense of self-identity with both individuals being able to express a clearly-developed sense of identity. It is about adaptation, cooperation, and alignment with another for the greater good of a union in which both people are enhanced by their participation in that relationship. A relationship is not working if one person consistently benefits from the relationship and the other subordinates his or her identity and direction in life.

Both individuals need to know themselves as contributors to one another and to their relationship. Dialogue and flow in such a relationship cannot spring from a vague sense of self. The intention to have a successful relationship originates out of a strong, aligned, self-identity. The needs of both individuals are assessed to promote the higher good of both. Subordinating your own will does not make you more flexible; it only makes your own will-based energy subordinate. The goal is not to be to be pliable at the cost of one's identity when accommodating another simply weakens you.

> *Strive for greater alignment between the Limited Self and the Eternal Self. This will result in an increase in your capacity for authentic, reciprocal relationships.*

Always adjusting does not signal a reciprocal relationship. The engine is being driven primarily by the personality wants and needs of the dominant partner. In order to make the relationship work in this situation, the will and vision of the other is increasingly weakened to the authority of the dominant partner or the relationship. This, then, is no longer a reciprocal relationship, but an unbalanced one in which domination and submission are themes rather than mutual strengths.

At the individual level, above all, you have to cultivate a relationship with yourself. You need to strive for clear self-identity and self-knowing. Such knowledge allows you to be pro-active and to create anew the relationships in your life. You have the ability to fashion a more vital, reciprocal relationship. This course will further cultivate a relationship between the Limited Self and the Eternal Self.

If you want to create a reciprocal relationship:

- You need to increase your self-knowledge.
- You need to cultivate friendship first, in any relationship.
- You need to broaden and expand what you are willing to give.
- You need to stop harboring resentments and grievances in on-going relationships.
- You need to see negotiation as tied to opportunity in self-discovery.
- You need to expand your view of your soul nature.

Going Deeper on Reciprocity

In your journal:

- Make a list of the significant family members and friends currently in your life. How many of these individuals have the capacity to participate in a reciprocal relationship? Are the people in your life capable and willing to do their share to make a relationship viable? Or do you have relationships that are notable for their one-sidedness.

- Are you usually in the role of the giver without asking much for yourself? Why? Could it be that you have some issues about your worthiness to receive? Is it a reflection of needing to give enough, or be perfect enough, to be loved? Are there other familiar themes that play old family refrains?

- Do you feel that, if you are loved, that you should be primarily in the position of receiving, with your needs getting first priority? Do you feel that you should not have to adjust significantly to give to others? Do you feel that subordinating your wants, needs, and desires restricts your freedom and your ability to be yourself?

- Do you believe your partner feels that, if he or she is loved, his or her needs should be the first priority? How do the two of you accommodate these different perspectives?

With one (1) being uncomfortable and (5) being very comfortable:

> How do you rate yourself as a giver?
> How do you rate yourself as a receiver?

Who is Incapable of a Reciprocal Relationship?

- A child in a parent-child relationship. The child is not a peer in a reciprocal relationship with an adult. It is not a reciprocal relationship because of the inherent dependency of the child. The role of the adult is not an equal, co-created role with a child.

- Narcissistic individual—A narcissist due to a variety of psychological and social problems is unable to take the world of the other into account over self-needs and self-gratification.

- People who are chemically-dependent or addicted to other behaviors such as gambling, sex, or control. The obsessive compulsive drive is greater than the capacity for relationship.
- Individuals who avoid, or are incapable of, admitting responsibility. Note: You should not believe in the power of anyone to change who will not acknowledge their accountability or responsibility.

On one level, reciprocity can be seen as the ability to go beyond the narrow interests of self in loving support of another human being, but in a larger context, reciprocity is the ability of the Limited Self to move into greater alignment with the Eternal Self. Reciprocity is based on the ability to feel the vibration of spirit within our own souls and to see that light and to feel that energy and know that truth about the soul of another. The nature of reciprocity is spiritual because it goes beyond ego-based self-interests and leads to a true union of two souls. The practice of going beyond self-interest on behalf of another creates greater alignment with our higher nature and is the true purpose of relationships.

EFFORT

Relationships flourish with effort. Effort is energized intention that creates forward movement. Forward movement is positive, projecting energy towards desired goals. You place intention on both your relationship with yourself and your relationship with other people. If your intention is to be authentic with yourself, capable of entering into self-dialogue and self-exploration, that intention will manifest by continuously re-energizing and refueling it.

{ *Intimacy is two souls touching.* }

Areas in which intention must precede effort include:
- Intention for an authentic relationship.
- Intention for greater alignment between the two selves.
- Intention to be trustworthy with self and with others.
- Intention to strive to make effort to create more in a relationship.

Key ideas regarding effort:
- Effort is energized intention directed by will.
- Consistent, sustained effort underpins deep, caring relationships.
- Effort strengthens and deepens self-discipline.
- Effort can be sustained and energized by rightful intention.
- The willingness to apply effort in a relationship is proof and evidence of the depth of commitment.

Romantic Love Also Requires Effort

In family relationships and in raising children, you may understand that, although there is love, the relationships are going to require work, effort and focus. But as you have seen, one of the relationship myths around romantic love is that good relationships can be achieved and sustained without work. This myth has its basis in a society that romanticizes immediate gains and devalues delayed gratification. The idea persists that if two people are meant to be together, they will just know it, feel it, and have it. Kismet and destiny do not resonate with the vibration of words like "work," "effort," "perseverance" and "discipline." The feeling state of love and caring is romanticized and the basis in friendship that allows for the continuation of relationship is frequently seen as unnecessary.

As you saw earlier, many people feel "This relationship shouldn't be this much work." The implication is that, if there is too much work, another relationship probably is better, or at least easier. What if God said that about us! The truth is you are a complex human being and different individuals have unsynchronized wants, needs, and desires. Applied effort is one of the only means by which deep friendship and deep love can be further deepened, developed, and cultivated.

Another idea around caring and romantic love is the idea that "I love someone, but I am no longer in love with them." That translates to the statement that "The initial high of attraction and romanticized projection has diminished with the passage of time." People often assume that a relationship will maintain at that level and that any requirement of steady applied effort, energy, analysis, reframing and restructuring will be unnecessary. Energy and effort are the harnessing of God's energy in motion and movement. Such effort is is not about drudgery, but rather presents an opportunity for disciplined creativity that has momentum, application, and force of intention.

SACRIFICE

Sacrifice involves the ability to forsake ego-based agendas on behalf of another, others, or a higher ideal. It is a moment of, or a pattern of, transcending personal motives, personal wants and desires, for that which is perceived as a greater good.

There may come a time when an individual whose life has been focused upon sacrifice may look back and question that choice or the decisions that resulted. The fact is at that moment in time when the sacrifice occurred, the higher self was reaching for a greater good to the best of that person's ability to assess

> *To sacrifice is to go beyond the wants, needs, and desires of the Limited Self and to participate in higher alignment with the Eternal Self.*

it at that moment. This capacity to sacrifice on behalf of another is the path of heroes, sages and saints, the embodiment of lofty ideals. This capacity is also within you.

Sacrifice is a complex subject. Individuals, or groups of individuals, may attempt to subordinate or coerce sacrifice by indoctrination to specific ideas or prescribed ideals. The history of wars and military pursuits often involve attempts to inspire sacrifice from soldiers and citizens, while at the same time attempting to subordinate the individual's right to assess, evaluate and align their mental and spiritual world to that which they perceive to be right.

Not all actions requested in the name of sacrifice are for the higher good. You should never suspend your right to evaluate, to discern, and to intuit just because you think those activities are ego-based—especially if coercion dismisses the exceptional qualities involved in evaluation, discernment and intuition, while calling for sacrifice. Hidden, or not-so-hidden agendas may be in play to nullify discernment and numb judgment by praising a false ideal of sacrifice. You should always be willing to sacrifice, but you should never suspend intuition and judgment in the holy name of sacrifice. That is not true sacrifice, but the movement of consciousness through indoctrination or brainwashing.

You have the capacity to transcend the narrow interests of the self. You also have the capacity to be manipulated by an ideal of sacrifice that is not a calling to a higher ideal but a calling to suspend judgment and agree to agendas for the political and personal gain of others. Living more consciously means going beyond embracing words and ideals without analysis and judgment. In his excellent book *Escape from Freedom*, Eric Fromm analyzes the psychology behind the rise of Nazism and the Second World War; he identifies man's willingness to commit to a larger cause in an effort to escape the terror of his own freedom and feelings of aloneness in the world.

In all relationships, there are times when efforts, responsibilities and duties are disproportionately handed out and need to be assumed. A reciprocal relationship has an underlying theme of the willingness to sacrifice on behalf of the relationship or on behalf of the welfare of another. Its merit is in the exchange of love in the dance of give-and-take; two individuals flow to the music of life and move in mutual support of one another.

Real sacrifice is an act of transcendence. You transcend the ego-based consciousness to achieve a higher level of spiritual participation. Sacrifice, when expressed in a relationship, allows that capacity to buoy up another. One person carries the weight of one who is burdened. It uplifts, not only by encouragement, but also by demonstration. It is a gift that validates the intrinsic worth of another and elevates the consciousness of self to another level of self-knowing and alignment with the divine. No sacrifice is ever lost for its worth is not in the acknowledgement, but in the doing. In the doing, the divine was exalted and man became more than he knew himself to be. Those around him were lifted and changed by the sacrifice.

In your myriad relationships you can only attempt to live in balance, with good will, positive intentions and rightful actions towards others. Still, there is no guarantee that, with the movement of the light and the shadow, crises will not disrupt the existing peace and harmony in your life. Since you are unable to control external events in the world, it is in your best interest to evaluate, assess and be clear about your meaningful relationships. Your intention and attention to building a relationship with yourself and with others will allow you to draw from the sustaining, loving flow of Spirit. You have the power to gain and regain the stability by which you are anchored to the earth, believing in the promise of the sunlight of another day. To insure that your relationships are satisfying, healthy and established in the highest principles of happiness, be someone who C.A.R.E.S.

Affirmations for C.A.R.E.S.

For Channeling Light and Love
I am a channel of light
reflecting the light of All.
I am a channel of love,
expressing the love of All.

For Empathy and Understanding
I am a friend to all.
Empathy and understanding
are my essence.
Love is my nature.

For Connecting in Love
I am centered
in the light and love connection
with myself.
I am whole
in my capacity to love others.
I am whole and complete
for I am connected
with myself and Spirit.

For Divine Radiance
I am divine light,
shining particles of God,
embraced by that light
which emanates from within me.

For Selfless Compassion

I am compassion.
I dissolve
into loving you
and merge
beyond boundaries
of knowing.

www.ingramcontent.com/pod-product-compliance
Lightning Source LLC
LaVergne TN
LVHW021600070426
835507LV00014B/1876